THIS BOOK BELONGS TO:

....

CHRISTMAS 2006

Christmas
with Southern Living
2006

Christmas
with Southern Living
2006

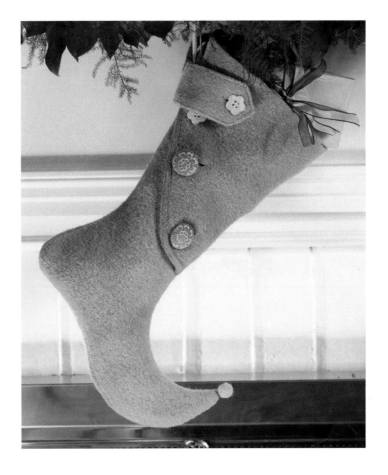

Edited by Rebecca Brennan and Julie Gunter

OXMOOR HOUSE.

©2006 by Oxmoor House, Inc.
Book Division of Southern Progress Corporation
P. O. Box 2262, Birmingham, Alabama 35201-2262

Southern Living® is a federally registered trademark belonging to
Southern Living, Inc.

ISBN-13: 978-0-8487-3115-1
ISBN-10: 0-8487-3115-8
ISSN: 0747-7791
Printed in the United States of America
First Printing 2006

Editor in Chief: Nancy Fitzpatrick Wyatt
Executive Editor: Susan Carlisle Payne
Copy Chief: Allison Long Lowery

Christmas with Southern Living® 2006
Editor: Rebecca Brennan
Foods Editor: Julie Gunter
Assistant Foods Editor: Julie Christopher
Senior Copy Editor: L. Amanda Owens
Copy Editor: Donna Baldone
Editorial Assistant: Brigette Gaucher
Senior Designer: Melissa Jones Clark
Photography Director: Jim Bathie
Senior Photo Stylist: Kay E. Clarke
Photo Stylist: Katherine Eckert
Director, Test Kitchens: Elizabeth Tyler Austin
Food Stylist: Kelley Self Wilton
Test Kitchens Staff: Kristi Carter, Nicole Lee Faber,
    Kathleen Royal Phillips, Elise Weis
Director of Production: Laura Lockhart
Publishing Systems Administrator: Rick Tucker
Senior Production Manager: Greg A. Amason
Production Assistant: Faye Porter Bonner

Contributors
Designer: Carol Damsky
Indexer: Mary Ann Laurens
Interns: Meg Kozinsky, Ashley Leath, Caroline Markunas,
    Vanessa Rusch Thomas
Photographer: Lee Harrelson

To order additional publications, call 1-800-765-6400, or
visit oxmoorhouse.com

Cover: White Chocolate Rice Pudding with Dried Cherry Sauce, page 32
Back cover, clockwise from top left: Chocolate-Espresso Pots de Crème,
page 42; Garden-Style Greetings, page 110; Holiday Martinis, page 78;
Triple Chocolate-Nut Clusters and White Chocolate-Peppermint Jumbles,
page 73

Contents

12 Menus of Christmas

Beef Tenderloin Repast. 12

Turkey and All the Trimmings. 18

An English Feast 23

Roasted Lamb Dinner. 26

A Southern Holiday Supper 30

Mother-Daughter Holiday Tea. 34

Tuscan Dinner Party 40

Vegetarian Night 44

Brunch Buffet. 48

Country Dinner. 53

Ham Dinner 56

Office Party 62

Season's Best Recipes

Our Best Casseroles 68

Slow-Cooker Sensations 72

Twice as Nice. 76

Seasonal Pantry Favorites 84

Share the Spirit of the Season

Wrapped in Style 164
Irresistible Invitations 166
Easy, Artsy Gift Tags 167

Where to Find It 168
Recipe Index 172
General Index 174
Contributors 175

Holiday Planner 177

Easy Ideas for Creative Decorating

A Mantel for Two Seasons 92
Retro Chic 98
Easy, Earthy Style 104
Garden-Style Greetings 110
Fresh Greens 118
Winsome Windows 124
Inspiration Point 130
Passion for Plates 134
Star Power 138
A Merry Welcome 144

Do-It-Yourself Holiday Style

Decorating Classics in 3 Easy Steps 148
Quick-as-a-Wink Centerpieces 152
Pillows with Pizzazz 158
Spotlight on Shades 160

12 Menus of Christmas

With this grand array of menus, you'll entertain with ease.
Time-saving game plans, make-ahead options, and over 80 recipes
give you everything you need to host the most memorable
gatherings of the season.

Beef Tenderloin Repast

Smoked Trout and Pecan Crostini

Baby Romaine and Blood Orange Salad

Bacon-Wrapped Beef Tenderloin with Madeira

Butternut Squash Mash   Balsamic Beans

Grilled Red Cabbage with Garlic Cream

Dark Chocolate Chunk Cherry Cake

serves 10

menu prep plan

3 days ahead:

• Cook butternut squash and garlic; prepare Butternut Squash Mash. Chill.

• Prepare smoked trout spread; chill. Toast baguette slices; store at room temperature in an airtight container.

2 days ahead:

• Section oranges and prepare vinaigrette for Baby Romaine and Blood Orange Salad; chill.

• Microwave cabbage wedges, and prepare Garlic Cream for Grilled Red Cabbage; chill.

1 day ahead:

• Prepare Dark Chocolate Chunk Cherry Cake.

• Prepare Bacon-Wrapped Tenderloin, but do not cook; cover and chill.

• Trim beans; chill.

2 hours ahead:

• Cook beef tenderloin, and prepare Madeira sauce; keep warm.

1 hour ahead:

• Grill cabbage wedges; arrange on a serving platter and keep warm.

• Arrange smoked trout and baguette slices on a serving plate.

30 minutes ahead:

• Reheat Butternut Squash Mash in microwave.

• Prepare and bake Balsamic Beans.

• Reheat Garlic Cream to serve with Grilled Red Cabbage.

• Slice tenderloin; arrange on a serving platter.

• Toss lettuce with remaining salad ingredients.

Shown on previous page: Warm Bean Salad with Olives (page 40), Chocolate-Espresso Pots de Crème (page 42)

make ahead

Smoked Trout and Pecan Crostini

Prep: 18 min.   Cook: 8 min.   Other: 1 hr.

1	(8-ounce) package smoked trout fillets, skinned and boned (about 2 fillets)
1	(8-ounce) package cream cheese, softened
½	cup chopped pecans, toasted
½	cup sour cream
1	shallot, quartered
2	teaspoons prepared horseradish
2	tablespoons fresh lemon juice
½	teaspoon freshly ground black pepper
¼	cup olive oil
2	teaspoons minced garlic
1	French baguette, sliced into ⅓" slices

Combine first 8 ingredients in a food processor; process until smooth. Chill 1 hour or up to 1 week. Serve at room temperature.

Combine olive oil and garlic; brush both sides of bread slices with garlic oil; arrange slices on baking sheets.

Bake at 400° for 8 minutes or until crisp and golden. Cool completely. Serve with spread. Yield: 2¾ cups.

Baby Romaine and Blood Orange Salad

Prep: 15 min.

5	blood oranges or red navel oranges
¼	cup sherry vinegar
2	tablespoons honey
2	tablespoons minced shallot (about 2 shallots)
1	tablespoon minced fresh thyme
½	teaspoon salt
½	teaspoon pepper
⅓	cup extra-virgin olive oil
10	cups baby Romaine lettuce (9 ounces)
½	cup pine nuts, toasted

Section oranges by cutting away the rind and white pith; carefully cut alongside each membrane to remove fruit, using a paring knife. Squeeze remaining membranes to extract juice. Combine juice, vinegar, and next 5 ingredients in a large bowl; slowly drizzle in oil while whisking constantly. Cover and chill up to 2 days (return to room temperature before serving).

Toss lettuce with orange segments, pine nuts, and desired amount of dressing. Serve immediately. Yield: 10 servings.

Baby Romaine and
Blood Orange Salad

Bacon-Wrapped Beef Tenderloin with Madeira, Balsamic Beans, Butternut Squash Mash, Grilled Red Cabbage with Garlic Cream

editor's favorite • make ahead

Bacon-Wrapped Beef Tenderloin with Madeira

Beef broth and consommé appear in tandem to give the Madeira reduction a richer flavor.

Prep: 31 min.   Cook: 1 hr.   Other: 10 min.

1   (6- to 6½-pound) beef tenderloin, trimmed
1   tablespoon freshly ground pepper, divided
1½   teaspoons salt
½   cup chopped fresh flat-leaf parsley, divided
¼   cup chopped fresh rosemary
¼   cup fresh thyme leaves, divided

1   pound bacon slices (about 20 slices) (we tested with Boar's Head)
⅓   cup minced shallots
2   (3.5-ounce) packages shiitake mushrooms, stems removed and sliced
2   (3.5-ounce) packages oyster mushrooms, stems removed and sliced
1   cup Madeira
1   (14-ounce) can beef broth or fat-free, less-sodium beef broth
1   (10½-ounce) can beef consommé, undiluted
3   tablespoons unsalted butter
Garnish: fresh herb sprigs

Cut tenderloin in half crosswise; sprinkle both pieces evenly with 2½ teaspoons pepper and salt. Combine ¼ cup parsley, rosemary, and 3 tablespoons thyme; rub over beef. Fold narrow end of tenderloin under to achieve a uniform thickness.

Wrap bacon around tenderloin pieces, and secure at 1" intervals with heavy string. Heat a 12" nonstick skillet over medium-high heat; add beef in 2 batches. Cook 8 to 10 minutes, turning often to brown all sides. Remove beef from pan, reserving 2 tablespoons drippings in skillet.

Place beef on a rack in a large roasting pan. Bake at 400° for 40 to 50 minutes or until a meat thermometer inserted into thickest part of tenderloin registers 140° (rare) to 160° (medium) or to desired degree of doneness. Remove tenderloin to a serving platter, and cover with aluminum foil; let stand 10 minutes before slicing. Remove string.

Meanwhile, heat reserved pan drippings in same skillet over medium-high heat; add shallots, mushrooms, and remaining 1 tablespoon thyme. Cook 3 minutes; add Madeira, stirring to loosen particles from bottom of pan. Add beef broth and consommé; bring to a boil. Boil 10 to 12 minutes or until reduced to about 3 cups. Remove from heat; add remaining ½ teaspoon pepper, remaining ¼ cup parsley, and butter, whisking until butter melts.

Slice tenderloin into ½"-thick slices; arrange on a serving platter. Garnish, if desired. Serve with Madeira sauce. Yield: 10 servings.

Make Ahead: Cover and refrigerate uncooked bacon-wrapped tenderloins up to 24 hours. Let stand at room temperature 30 minutes before proceeding with the recipe.

Wrap and tie tenderloin pieces to ready them for cooking.

editor's favorite • make ahead

Butternut Squash Mash

The subtle blend of sage and garlic enhances this yummy alternative to mashed potatoes.

Prep: 31 min.   Cook: 1 hr., 24 min.   Other: 10 min.

3	large butternut squash (about 3½ to 5¼ pounds each)
2	small garlic bulbs
1	tablespoon olive oil
2	tablespoons butter
½	cup half-and-half
1	tablespoon minced fresh sage
2	teaspoons salt
1	teaspoon freshly ground pepper

To make squash easier to cut, prick squash with a paring knife; microwave each squash on HIGH 4 to 5 minutes. Carefully cut squash in half lengthwise using a sharp chef's knife, discarding seeds and membranes. Line 2 large baking sheets with aluminum foil; lightly grease foil. Arrange squash halves, cut side down, on baking sheets.

Cut off pointed ends of garlic bulbs. Place garlic on a piece of aluminum foil, and drizzle with oil. Fold foil to seal; place on 1 baking sheet with squash.

Place 1 baking sheet on upper oven rack; 1 on lower oven rack. Bake at 350° for 1 hour, switching baking sheet positions after 35 minutes. Let cool 10 minutes.

Scoop out squash from shell, and place in a large bowl. Squeeze garlic cloves from bulbs; mash with a fork.

Melt butter in a small saucepan over medium heat. Stir in half-and-half and next 3 ingredients; bring to a simmer. Remove from heat.

Add herbed butter and mashed garlic to squash. Beat at medium speed with an electric mixer until smooth. Serve hot. Yield: 10 servings.

Make Ahead: Prepare squash mash. Cool, cover, and chill up to 3 days. Reheat Butternut Squash Mash loosely covered with heavy-duty plastic wrap in the microwave on HIGH 6 to 8 minutes or until heated thoroughly, stirring after 4 minutes, or bake it in a covered casserole dish at 350° until hot.

Balsamic Beans

A quick-to-make balsamic syrup enhances these roasted green beans. The balsamic syrup's also good drizzled over pork roast or even sliced fresh strawberries.

Prep: 6 min.   Cook: 27 min.

½   cup balsamic vinegar
2½   pounds green beans, trimmed
2   tablespoons olive oil
1   teaspoon salt
½   teaspoon freshly ground pepper

Cook vinegar in a small saucepan over medium heat 9 minutes or until syrupy and reduced to 3 tablespoons; set aside.

Toss beans with oil in a large bowl. Spread beans on a large rimmed baking sheet; sprinkle with salt and pepper.

Bake at 475° for 15 to 18 minutes or until charred in appearance (do not stir). Toss hot beans with balsamic syrup. Serve immediately. Yield: 10 servings.

Fix it Faster: Purchase prewashed, trimmed green beans available in the produce department.

Make Ahead: The balsamic syrup can be made a day ahead and stored at room temperature. Make a few extra batches of the syrup and consider it for gift giving.

editor's favorite • make ahead

Grilled Red Cabbage with Garlic Cream

Give yourself some extra time by following the make-ahead tips in the recipe. We also give an indoor cooking option that produces similar results.

Prep: 10 min.   Cook: 24 min.

2   small heads red cabbage (about 3 pounds)
2   tablespoons water
2   tablespoons butter or margarine
1   tablespoon minced garlic, divided (about 3 cloves)
1   cup heavy whipping cream
¾   teaspoon salt, divided
¾   teaspoon freshly ground pepper, divided
¼   cup olive oil

Remove outer leaves, and cut each cabbage head into 6 wedges, leaving core portion attached to hold the wedges together. Place wedges in a large glass bowl; add 2 tablespoons water, and cover loosely with heavy-duty plastic wrap. Microwave at HIGH for 9 minutes or until tender. (For

make ahead: Arrange cabbage wedges on a jelly-roll pan, and refrigerate to cool quickly and stop the cooking process. Cover and chill up to 2 days.)

Meanwhile, melt butter in a small saucepan over medium heat; add 1 teaspoon garlic, and sauté 1 minute or until garlic is golden. Add cream, and bring to a boil. Reduce heat, and simmer over medium-low heat 10 minutes or until slightly thickened. Add ¼ teaspoon each of salt and pepper. (For make ahead: Cover garlic cream, and chill up to 2 days; reheat in microwave or saucepan.)

Combine olive oil and remaining 2 teaspoons minced garlic in a small bowl; brush oil over cabbage wedges. Sprinkle cabbage with remaining ½ teaspoon each of salt and pepper. Grill, covered with grill lid, over medium-high heat (350° to 400°) 12 minutes or until browned and slightly charred, turning once. Arrange cabbage on a serving platter; drizzle each wedge with about 1 tablespoon garlic cream. Yield: 12 servings.

Indoor Cooking Option: Broil steamed cabbage on ungreased baking sheets 5½ inches from heat 24 minutes or until browned and slightly charred, turning once.

editor's favorite

Dark Chocolate Chunk Cherry Cake

Prep: 20 min.   Cook: 1 hr., 4 min.   Other: 18 min.

Unsweetened cocoa
1   (18.25-ounce) package yellow cake mix with pudding
½   cup sugar
1   (3.8-ounce) package devil's food instant pudding mix
4   large eggs
¾   cup vegetable oil
½   cup water
1   (8-ounce) container sour cream
1   tablespoon vanilla extract
5   (3-ounce) dark chocolate bars, divided (we tested with Ghirardelli)
½   cup coarsely chopped dried cherries
1   tablespoon butter
⅓   cup heavy whipping cream

Grease a 12-cup Bundt pan, and dust with cocoa; set aside.

Combine cake mix, sugar, and pudding mix in a large mixing bowl.

Beat eggs and next 4 ingredients at medium speed with an electric mixer until blended. Gradually add oil mixture to dry ingredients; beat 2 minutes. Coarsely chop 3 chocolate bars; fold cherries and chopped chocolate into batter. Pour batter into prepared pan.

Dark Chocolate Chunk Cherry Cake

Dried cherries and dark chocolate transform cake mix into this ultra decadent dessert.

Bake at 350° for 1 hour or until a wooden pick inserted in center comes out clean. Cool cake in pan on a wire rack 15 minutes. Remove from pan; cool completely on wire rack.

Coarsely chop 1 chocolate bar. Place chopped chocolate and butter in a small bowl; set aside.

Bring whipping cream to a simmer in a small saucepan over medium-high heat. Remove from heat, and immediately pour over chocolate and butter. Whisk gently until smooth. Cool glaze 3 minutes or until slightly thickened. Drizzle glaze over cake. Coarsely chop remaining chocolate bar; sprinkle chopped chocolate over cake. Yield: 12 servings.

Turkey and All the Trimmings

Cauliflower Bisque

Green Salad with Cranberry-Champagne Vinaigrette

Roast Turkey with Cider-Rosemary Gravy

Roasted Garlic and Herb Potatoes

Green Beans with Roasted Shallots

Ginger-Rum Carrots

Caramel Chess Tart

serves 10

menu prep plan

4 days ahead:
- Place turkey in refrigerator to thaw, if frozen.
- Toast seasoned pecans for salad; place in airtight container.
- Roast garlic for potatoes; chill.

1 day ahead:
- Prepare Cranberry-Champagne Vinaigrette; chill.
- Trim green beans, and cook; chill.
- Slice carrots; chill.
- Prepare Caramel Chess Tart; cover and store at room temperature.
- Prepare Cauliflower Bisque; chill.

4 to 5 hours ahead:
- Whip cream for Caramel Chess Tart; chill.
- Combine ingredients for salad except oranges, vinaigrette, and pecans; chill.
- Bake turkey; keep warm.
- Prepare Roasted Garlic and Herb Potatoes; keep warm.

1 hour ahead:
- Prepare Ginger-Rum Carrots; keep warm.
- Complete preparation of Green Beans with Roasted Shallots; keep warm.
- Prepare Cider-Rosemary Gravy; keep warm.

last minute:
- Reheat Cauliflower Bisque.
- Carve turkey.
- Add oranges, pecans, and vinaigrette to green salad.

Cauliflower Bisque

To preserve the creamy white color of this soup, sauté the veggies just until soft, but not browned.

Prep: 32 min.   Cook: 45 min.

3	tablespoons butter or margarine
2	cups chopped leeks
1	cup chopped celery
3	garlic cloves, chopped
8	cups cauliflower florets and stems (about 2 small heads)
6¾	cups chicken broth, divided
1	cup half-and-half
½	teaspoon salt
¼	teaspoon ground white pepper

Garnishes: croutons, fresh chives

Melt butter in a Dutch oven over medium heat. Add leeks, celery, and garlic; sauté 10 minutes or until vegetables are tender, but not brown. Add cauliflower; sauté 2 minutes. Add 6 cups broth; bring to a boil. Reduce heat, and simmer, uncovered, 20 minutes, or until vegetables are very tender. Cool slightly.

Puree vegetables, in batches, in a blender or food processor until very smooth and creamy. Return pureed vegetables to pan. Stir in half-and-half, salt, and pepper. Bring soup to a simmer over medium heat. Stir in remaining ¾ cup broth, and cook 5 minutes or until thoroughly heated. Garnish, if desired. Yield: about 10 cups.

Use your glitzy ornaments as place card holders.

Roast Turkey with Cider-Rosemary Gravy,
Roasted Garlic and Herb Potatoes,
Green Beans with Roasted Shallots,
Ginger-Rum Carrots

Green Salad with Cranberry-Champagne Vinaigrette

The savory nuts that top these greens can be made up to a week in advance and kept in an airtight container.

Prep: 8 min. Cook: 15 min.

2   cups pecan halves
3   tablespoons butter, melted
1   teaspoon paprika
1   teaspoon garlic powder
1   teaspoon onion powder
1   teaspoon salt
1   cup whole-berry cranberry sauce
½   cup cranberry juice
2   tablespoons champagne vinegar
½   teaspoon salt
¼   teaspoon freshly ground black pepper
½   cup extra-virgin olive oil
3   (5-ounce) packages mixed salad greens (we tested with Dole Spring Mix)
⅓   cup chopped fresh flat-leaf parsley
1   small red onion, thinly sliced
2   navel oranges, peeled and sectioned, or 1 cup drained mandarin oranges

Combine first 6 ingredients in a small bowl; toss well. Arrange pecans in a single layer on a foil-lined baking sheet. Bake at 350° for 15 minutes or until toasted; set aside.

Combine cranberry sauce and next 4 ingredients in a jar with a tight-fitting lid; shake well until cranberry sauce dissolves. Add oil; shake well.

Combine greens, parsley, onion, and oranges; toss well. Sprinkle with reserved pecans, and serve with desired amount of vinaigrette. Yield: 10 servings.

editor's favorite

Roast Turkey with Cider-Rosemary Gravy

This turkey gets basted in apple cider, giving it a wonderfully caramelized skin.

Prep: 39 min. Cook: 3 hrs., 15 min.

1   (16-pound) fresh or frozen turkey, thawed
1   teaspoon salt
1   teaspoon pepper
1   large onion, coarsely chopped
2   celery ribs, coarsely chopped
1   Golden Delicious apple, coarsely chopped
3   fresh rosemary sprigs
2   tablespoons butter, softened
6   center-cut bacon slices
1¼   cups apple cider, divided
2   tablespoons finely chopped onion
1   garlic clove, minced
2   teaspoons minced fresh rosemary
2   tablespoons all-purpose flour
¼   teaspoon salt
¼   teaspoon pepper
Garnish: rosemary sprigs

Remove giblets and neck, and rinse turkey with cold water; pat dry. Sprinkle cavity with 1 teaspoon salt and 1 teaspoon pepper. Place turkey, breast side up, in a roasting pan. Lightly stuff turkey body cavity with coarsely chopped onion, celery, apple, and 3 rosemary sprigs. Rub turkey with butter.

Loosen skin from turkey breast without totally detaching skin; carefully slip bacon slices under skin. Replace skin, using wooden picks to fasten skin over breast meat. Tie ends of legs together with heavy string, or tuck under flap of skin. Lift wing tips up and over back, and tuck under bird. Pour ¾ cup apple cider over turkey.

Bake turkey, uncovered, at 450° for 20 minutes. Reduce heat to 350°; bake 2 hours and 45 minutes or until a meat thermometer inserted into meaty part of thigh registers 180°, basting often with pan juices. Shield turkey with heavy-duty aluminum foil during cooking, if necessary, to prevent over-browning.

Transfer turkey to a serving platter; cover loosely with foil. Scrape roasting pan to remove browned bits; pour pan drippings into a gravy separator. Discard fat, reserving 2 tablespoons.

Heat reserved 2 tablespoons fat in a small saucepan over medium-high heat. Add finely chopped onion, garlic, and 2 teaspoons rosemary; sauté 2 minutes or until tender. Reduce heat to medium; add flour, and cook 1 minute. Whisk in pan drippings and remaining ½ cup cider. Bring to a boil; reduce heat, and simmer 2 to 3 minutes or until gravy thickens. Stir in ¼ teaspoon salt and ¼ teaspoon pepper. Serve gravy with turkey. Garnish, if desired. Yield: 16 servings.

Note: For ease in removing hot turkey from roasting pan, wear clean heat-resistant rubber gloves. They shield the heat and enable you to get a firm grip on the bird.

Roasted Garlic and Herb Potatoes

Roasted garlic can be made ahead for this dish and stored in a zip-top bag in the refrigerator up to a week.

Prep: 47 min.   Cook: 2 hrs., 30 min.   Other: 10 min.

5   large garlic bulbs
2   tablespoons olive oil
1½   cups milk
1½   cups heavy whipping cream
1   tablespoon salt
2   teaspoons freshly ground black pepper
¼   teaspoon ground nutmeg
4½   pounds baking potatoes
½   cup chopped fresh sage leaves
½   cup chopped fresh oregano
1½   cups freshly grated Parmesan cheese

Cut off pointed end of each garlic bulb; place garlic on a piece of aluminum foil, and drizzle with oil. Fold foil to seal. Bake at 350° for 1 hour or until very soft; cool. Squeeze pulp from garlic bulbs to measure ¾ cup. Reserve any remaining garlic for another use. Process ¾ cup garlic, milk, and next 4 ingredients in a blender or food processor until smooth; transfer to a large bowl.

Peel potatoes and slice very thinly. Add potatoes to milk mixture as they are sliced. (This keeps potatoes from changing color.) Layer one-third each of potato mixture, herbs, and cheese in a greased 13" x 9" baking dish. Repeat layers twice, ending with cheese. Bake, covered, at 350° for 45 minutes. Uncover and bake 45 more minutes or until browned and bubbly. Let stand 10 minutes before serving. Yield: 12 servings.

Green Beans with Roasted Shallots

Prep: 29 min.   Cook: 44 min.

2½   pounds fresh green beans, trimmed
1   pound shallots, peeled and halved (about 4 cups)
¼   cup olive oil
1½   teaspoons kosher salt
1   teaspoon freshly ground pepper

Cook green beans in boiling, salted water 7 to 9 minutes or until crisp-tender. Plunge beans into ice water to stop the cooking process; drain and set aside.

Spread shallots in a single layer on an ungreased jelly-roll pan. Drizzle with olive oil; toss well to coat. Bake at 450° for 35 minutes or until shallots are roasted, stirring twice.

Combine beans, salt, and pepper in a large serving bowl; add roasted shallots and pan drippings; toss well. Serve warm or at room temperature. Yield: 10 servings.

Fix it Faster: You can find trimmed ready-to-eat green beans in the produce section of your grocery store.

editor's favorite
Ginger-Rum Carrots

A splash of rum and ginger-infused broth make these thick-sliced carrots some of the best we've tried.

Prep: 35 min.   Cook: 27 min.

7   cups chicken broth
½   cup sugar
1   (2-inch) piece fresh ginger, peeled and sliced into 6 pieces
4   pounds carrots, cut diagonally into ½" slices
½   cup butter
¼   cup finely chopped onion
2   tablespoons minced fresh ginger
2   teaspoons minced garlic
½   teaspoon salt
¼   teaspoon freshly ground black pepper
¼   cup spiced rum or dark rum (optional)
½   teaspoon vanilla extract

Combine first 3 ingredients in a Dutch oven; bring to a boil. Add carrots; reduce heat, and simmer, uncovered, 12 minutes or until almost tender. Drain; discard ginger slices. Set carrots aside.

Melt butter in a large skillet over medium heat. Add onion, minced ginger, and garlic; sauté 2 to 3 minutes or until onion is tender. Add reserved carrot, salt, and pepper; sauté 3 more minutes. Stir in rum, if desired, and vanilla; cook 1 minute. Yield: 10 servings.

Make Ahead: Place sliced carrots in a zip-top plastic bag, and store in refrigerator up to 2 days. Or for extra convenience, use packaged baby carrots.

Caramel Chess Tart

editor's favorite · make ahead

Caramel Chess Tart

Brown sugar and butter come together in this recipe to create a sublime caramel. This dessert's made of simple ingredients, yet it received our Test Kitchens highest marks.

Prep: 17 min. Cook: 54 min.

½   (15-ounce) package refrigerated piecrusts
½   cup butter, softened
1½ cups firmly packed light brown sugar
3   large eggs
1   tablespoon all-purpose flour
¼   cup buttermilk
2   teaspoons vanilla extract
Powdered sugar (optional)
Whipped cream

Fit piecrust into a 10" tart pan with a removable bottom according to package directions. Line pastry with aluminum foil, and fill with dried beans. Bake at 450° for 7 minutes. Remove dried beans and foil, and bake piecrust 2 more minutes; cool on a wire rack. Reduce oven temperature to 350°.

Beat butter and brown sugar in a large bowl at medium speed with an electric mixer until fluffy; add eggs, 1 at a time, beating well after each addition. Stir in flour and buttermilk. Add vanilla, stirring well. Pour filling into prepared crust.

Bake at 350° for 45 minutes or until almost set. Cool completely on wire rack. Remove tart pan rim and transfer tart to a serving platter. Dust with powdered sugar, if desired. Dollop each serving with whipped cream. Yield: 1 (10") tart.

Caramel Chess Tassies: To make 3 dozen tassies, prepare filling as directed above. You'll need 1½ (15-ounce) packages refrigerated piecrusts. Using a 2¾" round cutter, cut 36 circles out of piecrusts. Place in ungreased miniature muffin pans, crimping edges. Spoon filling evenly into crusts. Bake at 350° for 25 minutes. Remove from pans, and cool completely on wire racks. Yield: 3 dozen.

An English Feast

Potato-Leek Soup

Prime Rib with Horseradish Cream

Blue Cheese Yorkshire Puddings

Carrot Puree with Browned Butter and Ginger

Chocolate Bread Pudding

serves 8 to 10

menu prep plan

1 day ahead:

• Prepare Chocolate Bread Pudding, but do not bake.

• Prepare Potato-Leek Soup; chill.

• Prepare Carrot Puree with Browned Butter and Ginger; chill.

3 hours ahead:

• Prepare Prime Rib; keep warm.

• Prepare Horseradish Cream; chill.

1 hour ahead:

• Prepare Blue Cheese Yorkshire Puddings.

• Reheat Potato-Leek Soup in microwave.

• Reheat Carrot Puree with Browned Butter and Ginger in microwave.

last minute:

• Carve Prime Rib; arrange on serving platter with Yorkshire Puddings.

during dinner:

• Sprinkle morsels and pecans over Chocolate Bread Pudding; bake.

Prime Rib with
Horseradish Cream

Blue Cheese Yorkshire
Puddings

Potato-Leek Soup

For easy cleanup, use an immersion blender to puree soup right in the pan.

Prep: 10 min.   Cook: 1 hr., 25 min.

1	tablespoon butter
3	large leeks, trimmed and thinly sliced
2	large russet potatoes, peeled and cubed (about 2¼ pounds)
¾	cup dry white wine, divided
4	cups chicken broth
1	bay leaf
2	fresh thyme sprigs
2	fresh parsley sprigs
1	cup whipping cream
¾	teaspoon salt
¾	teaspoon freshly ground black pepper
2	tablespoons chopped fresh chives

Garnishes: fresh thyme or parsley sprigs

Melt butter in a large Dutch oven over medium-high heat; add leeks, and sauté 10 minutes or until tender. Add potato, ½ cup wine, and broth. Using a piece of kitchen twine, tie bay leaf, 2 thyme sprigs, and 2 parsley sprigs into a bundle; add to pan. Bring to a boil; reduce heat, and simmer, uncovered, 1 hour and 15 minutes or until potatoes are very tender. Discard herb bundle.

Process potato mixture, in batches, in a blender or food processor until smooth, stopping to scrape down sides. Return puree to Dutch oven. Add remaining ¼ cup wine, cream, and next 3 ingredients. Garnish, if desired. Yield: 8 cups.

Prime Rib with Horseradish Cream

English mustard is an extremely hot condiment containing ground mustard seeds and turmeric. It contributes high flavor to the coating that bakes on the prime rib.

Prep: 5 min. Cook: 2 hrs., 35 min. Other: 10 min.

2   tablespoons prepared English mustard (we tested with Colman's)
2   tablespoons prepared horseradish
1   tablespoon chopped fresh thyme
1   teaspoon salt
1   teaspoon pepper
1   (8½-pound) prime rib roast
Horseradish Cream
Garnishes: lady apples, kumquats, pecans

Combine first 5 ingredients; rub on all surfaces of roast. Place roast on a rack in a roasting pan.

Bake, uncovered, at 450° for 20 minutes. Reduce heat to 300°, and bake 2 hours and 15 minutes or until a meat thermometer inserted in thickest portion registers 145° (medium rare) or 160° (medium). Let stand 10 minutes before slicing. Transfer roast to a serving platter, reserving ¼ cup drippings for Blue Cheese Yorkshire Puddings; keep warm. Serve with Horseradish Cream. Garnish, if desired. Yield: 10 servings.

Horseradish Cream

Prep: 7 min.

1   cup heavy whipping cream
2   tablespoons finely chopped chives
2   tablespoons prepared horseradish
2   teaspoons prepared English mustard
½   teaspoon salt

Beat whipping cream at medium-high speed with an electric mixer until soft peaks form. Fold in chives and remaining ingredients. Cover and chill until ready to serve. Serve with Prime Rib. Yield: 2 cups.

Blue Cheese Yorkshire Puddings

Prep: 14 min. Cook: 40 min.

2   cups all-purpose flour
2   cups milk
1   teaspoon salt
5   large eggs, lightly beaten
4   ounces Stilton cheese, crumbled
¼   cup pan drippings from Prime Rib with Horseradish Cream

Preheat oven to 400°.

Whisk together first 4 ingredients until smooth; stir in crumbled cheese.

Place ungreased popover pans in preheated oven for 5 minutes. Brush bottom and sides of pans with pan drippings. Pour batter evenly into pans using a ladle. Bake at 400° for 35 minutes or until puffed and brown. Yield: 1 dozen.

Carrot Puree with Browned Butter and Ginger

Prep: 13 min. Cook: 28 min.

2½   pounds carrots, peeled and coarsely chopped
1   medium baking potato, peeled and coarsely chopped
¼   cup butter
⅔   cup half-and-half
1   teaspoon salt
1   teaspoon ground ginger
¼   teaspoon pepper
1   tablespoon white wine vinegar

Place carrot and potato in a large saucepan; add water to cover. Bring to a boil; cover, reduce heat, and simmer 25 minutes or until very tender. Drain well. Process half of potato and carrot in a food processor until smooth.

Place butter in a small skillet. Cook over medium heat 3 minutes or until butter solids turn light brown, stirring often. Add brown butter and half-and-half to carrot puree. Add remaining half of carrot and potato, salt, and remaining ingredients; process until smooth. Yield: 8 to 10 servings.

Note: Beurre noisette is French meaning " browned butter." Don't be tempted to substitute margarine; it won't have the same flavor or consistency. Cook carefully to develop the light hazelnut ("noisette") color.

Chocolate Bread Pudding

make ahead

Chocolate Bread Pudding

Prep: 12 min.   Cook: 1 hr., 20 min.   Other: 8 hrs., 10 min.

1   pound challah bread, torn into bite-size pieces*
3   tablespoons butter, softened and divided
4   cups half-and-half
1   (12-ounce) package semisweet chocolate morsels, divided
½   cup unsweetened cocoa
1½   cups sugar
½   teaspoon salt
5   large eggs, lightly beaten
¾   cup bourbon, half-and-half, or brewed coffee
1   cup coarsely chopped pecans

Place bread on 2 baking sheets, and bake at 325° for 12 minutes. Transfer bread to a large bowl, and set aside.

Butter a 13" x 9" baking dish with 1 tablespoon butter.

Bring half-and-half and remaining 2 tablespoons butter to a simmer in a large saucepan over medium-high heat. Remove from heat; add 1 cup chocolate morsels, stirring until melted. Whisk in cocoa and next 4 ingredients. Pour over bread, tossing to coat; transfer to baking dish. Cover and chill 8 hours.

Sprinkle with remaining chocolate morsels and pecans. Bake, uncovered, at 350° for 1 hour or until set. Let stand 10 minutes. Yield: 12 servings.

*You can use French bread as a substitute for challah.

Note: You can also bake bread pudding in 8 (8-ounce) ramekins or 12 (6-ounce) ramekins or custard cups. Prepare as directed above, and after chilling 8 hours, spoon pudding evenly into ramekins. Sprinkle with morsels and pecans. Bake, uncovered, at 350° for 35 minutes (for 6 ounce) to 40 minutes (for 8 ounce).

Roasted Lamb Dinner

Cornmeal-Crusted Oysters with Red Pepper Romesco

Roasted Mushroom Salad

Sage-Crusted Leg of Lamb with Pineapple-Pecan Salsa

Lemon Orzo

Wilted Kale with Roasted Garlic

Almond Torte with Cranberry Jam

serves 8

menu prep plan

3 days ahead:

- Prepare Red Pepper Romesco; chill.
- Prepare vinaigrette for mushroom salad; chill.

1 to 2 days ahead:

- Roast garlic; trim and slice kale for Wilted Kale with Roasted Garlic; chill separately.
- Prepare Pineapple-Pecan Salsa, but do not add pecans; chill.
- Cook orzo for Lemon Orzo; chill.
- Prepare Cranberry Jam and Almond Torte, but do not dust with powdered sugar; chill both.

2 to 3 hours ahead:

- Prepare Sage-Crusted Leg of Lamb; bake 2 hours before serving. Keep warm.

1½ hours ahead:

- Prepare Wilted Kale with Roasted Garlic; stir in roasted garlic and seasonings just before serving.
- Roast mushrooms for salad; cool to room temperature.

1 hour ahead:

- Slice lemons and fry Cornmeal-Crusted Oysters; keep warm.
- Complete preparation of Lemon Orzo.
- Place Red Pepper Romesco in serving dish.

last minute:

- Assemble Roasted Mushroom Salad on salad plates; whisk vinaigrette and serve.
- Stir pecans into Pineapple-Pecan Salsa.
- Carve lamb.
- Dust Almond Torte with powdered sugar before serving.

Sage-Crusted Leg of Lamb with Pineapple-Pecan Salsa, Wilted Kale with Roasted Garlic, Lemon Orzo

Cornmeal-Crusted Oysters with Red Pepper Romesco

Romesco, the classic Spanish sauce of tomatoes and red peppers, focuses solely on red peppers here and replaces the typical almonds with pecans, the South's prized nut. It's a perfect accompaniment with crusty fried oysters.

Prep: 19 min.   Cook: 15 min.

Peanut oil
1   cup yellow cornmeal
2½   teaspoons paprika
24   large fresh Select oysters, drained
1½   teaspoons salt, divided
Red Pepper Romesco
Lemon wedges

Pour oil to a depth of 1" into a large skillet; heat to 375°.

Meanwhile, combine cornmeal and paprika in a shallow dish. Sprinkle oysters with ½ teaspoon salt. Dip oysters in cornmeal mixture, pressing gently to coat.

Fry oysters, 4 to 6 at a time, 30 seconds on each side or until golden brown. Drain on paper towels. Serve oysters with Red Pepper Romesco and lemon wedges. Yield: 8 servings.

Red Pepper Romesco

Prep: 10 min.

¾ cup chopped pecans
6 garlic cloves
1 ancho chile, seeded and coarsely chopped
1 (12-ounce) jar roasted red bell peppers, drained
2 tablespoons red wine vinegar
2 tablespoons fresh flat-leaf parsley
½ teaspoon salt
¼ cup olive oil

Process first 3 ingredients in a food processor 30 seconds or until finely chopped. Add peppers and next 3 ingredients. With processor running, slowly pour oil through food chute in a thin stream. Pour into a bowl; cover and chill up to 3 days. Serve at room temperature. Yield: 1⅔ cups.

Roasted Mushroom Salad

Prep: 37 min.   Cook: 45 min.

2 (8-ounce) packages fresh mushrooms, quartered
2 (8-ounce) packages fresh crimini mushrooms, quartered
4 (3.5-ounce) packages fresh shiitake mushrooms, stemmed and quartered
3 tablespoons olive oil
½ teaspoon salt
⅓ cup sherry vinegar
2 tablespoons minced shallot
1 small garlic clove, pressed
2 teaspoons Dijon mustard
½ teaspoon salt
¼ teaspoon freshly ground pepper
⅔ cup olive oil
1 (5-ounce) package fresh baby spinach (about 6 cups)
1 small head fresh radicchio, torn (about 4 cups)
8 ounces crumbled blue cheese

Combine first 5 ingredients in a large roasting pan. Roast at 450° for 45 minutes or until liquid evaporates; stir twice.

Meanwhile, combine vinegar and next 5 ingredients in a small bowl with a wire whisk; slowly whisk in ⅔ cup oil.

Combine mushrooms and ¼ cup vinaigrette; cool to room temperature. Divide spinach and radicchio among serving plates; top with mushrooms and cheese. Drizzle with remaining dressing. Serve immediately. Yield: 8 servings.

Make Ahead: Chill the vinaigrette in a jar up to 3 days; whisk well before serving.

Sage-Crusted Leg of Lamb with Pineapple-Pecan Salsa

Kosher salt is a coarse-grained salt. Many prefer its chunky texture over regular table salt.

Prep: 10 min.   Cook: 1 hr., 30 min.   Other: 10 min.

2 tablespoons chopped fresh sage
2 tablespoons olive oil
1 teaspoon kosher salt
½ teaspoon freshly ground pepper
1 (5- to 6-pound) bone-in leg of lamb
4 garlic cloves, thinly sliced
Pineapple-Pecan Salsa

Combine first 4 ingredients in a small bowl.

Cut about 16 slits (about ½" deep) into lamb; insert garlic slices and a small amount of seasoned oil into each slit. Rub remaining oil over entire surface of lamb.

Place lamb on a rack in a roasting pan. Insert a meat thermometer into thickest part of roast, making sure it does not touch bone or fat.

Bake at 500° for 20 minutes; reduce temperature to 300°, and bake 1 hour and 10 minutes or until thermometer registers 150° (medium rare) or 160° (medium). Let stand 10 minutes. Slice lamb diagonally across the grain. Serve with Pineapple-Pecan Salsa. Yield: 8 servings.

Pineapple-Pecan Salsa

Prep: 19 min.   Cook: 10 min.

½ cup chopped onion
2 tablespoons olive oil
2 garlic cloves, minced
½ cup pineapple juice
4 cups finely chopped fresh pineapple
2 tablespoons chopped fresh sage
¼ teaspoon dried crushed red pepper (optional)
Pinch of salt
¾ cup chopped pecans, toasted

Sauté onion in olive oil in a medium skillet over medium heat 5 minutes or until tender. Add garlic; cook 1 minute, stirring constantly. Add pineapple juice; cook over medium-high heat until liquid is reduced by half (about 3 minutes).

Combine pineapple and next 3 ingredients in a large bowl; stir in onion mixture. Cover and chill up to 24 hours. Stir in pecans just before serving. Yield: 4 cups.

Fix it Faster: Start with a cored fresh pineapple to speed things up when making this salsa.

editor's favorite · *quick & easy*

editor's favorite · *quick & easy*

Lemon Orzo

Greek pasta is tossed with a warm, buttery blend of lemon and Parmesan.

Prep: 5 min. Cook: 18 min.

6	cups chicken broth
16	ounces uncooked orzo (rice-shaped pasta)
¼	cup butter or margarine
2	tablespoons grated fresh lemon rind
2	tablespoons fresh lemon juice
1½	cups freshly grated Parmesan cheese
½	teaspoon freshly ground pepper

Garnish: freshly grated Parmesan cheese

Bring broth to a boil in a Dutch oven. Stir in orzo; cook, uncovered, 9 to 11 minutes or until tender, stirring occasionally to prevent sticking. Drain.

Melt butter in same pan over medium heat. Add hot cooked orzo, lemon rind, and next 3 ingredients. Stir gently just until cheese melts. Serve hot. Garnish, if desired. Yield: about 7 cups.

Fix it Faster: Use refrigerated shredded Parmesan cheese.

Wilted Kale with Roasted Garlic

Prep: 21 min. Cook: 1 hr.

1	large garlic bulb
4	pounds kale, coarse stems removed (about 6 bunches)
¼	cup olive oil
¾	cup chicken broth
½	teaspoon salt
¼	teaspoon pepper

Cut off pointed end of garlic bulb. Place on a piece of aluminum foil, and coat generously with cooking spray. Fold foil to seal. Bake at 350° for 1 hour or until garlic is tender. Remove garlic from oven, and let cool. Squeeze pulp from garlic bulb, and mash with a fork until smooth. Set aside.

Meanwhile, slice kale leaves into ¼" strips. Heat olive oil in a large Dutch oven over medium heat. Gradually add kale, and cook 12 minutes or until kale wilts, stirring often. Add broth. Reduce heat to low; cover and simmer 20 to 25 minutes or until greens are tender and liquid evaporates. Stir in garlic, salt, and pepper. Yield: 8 servings.

Make Ahead: Roast garlic, and trim and slice kale up to 2 days ahead. Chill in separate zip-top plastic bags.

editor's favorite · *make ahead*

Almond Torte with Cranberry Jam

This moist, dense European-style cake is rich enough to serve without the jam, but don't forget the coffee.

Prep: 12 min. Cook: 1 hr.

12	ounces pure almond paste, crumbled (we tested with Odense)
¾	cup butter, softened
1¼	cups granulated sugar
4	large eggs
2	tablespoons almond liqueur
1¼	cups all-purpose flour
1	teaspoon baking powder

Powdered sugar
Cranberry Jam

Lightly grease and line bottom of a 9" springform pan with parchment paper; set aside.

Beat almond paste, butter, and granulated sugar at medium speed with a heavy-duty stand mixer until blended. Add eggs, 1 at a time, beating until blended after each addition. Beat in liqueur.

Combine flour and baking powder; add to butter mixture, beating at low speed just until blended. Spread batter into prepared pan.

Bake at 325° for 1 hour or until cake is golden and edges spring back when lightly touched. Cool completely in pan on a wire rack. Dust cake with powdered sugar, and serve with Cranberry Jam. Yield: 1 (9") cake.

gift idea · *make ahead* · *quick & easy*

Cranberry Jam

This jewel-toned jam can dress up vanilla ice cream, too.

Prep: 3 min. Cook: 10 min.

1	(12-ounce) package fresh cranberries
1	cup firmly packed light brown sugar
1	tablespoon grated orange rind
¼	cup fresh orange juice
2	tablespoons almond liqueur

Combine first 4 ingredients in a medium saucepan. Cook over medium heat 10 minutes or until thickened; stir in liqueur. Cool completely. Serve at room temperature or chilled. Yield: 1½ cups.

Make Ahead: Both the torte and the cranberry jam can be made a day ahead and chilled until ready to serve.

Almond Torte with Cranberry Jam

A Southern Holiday Supper

Oyster Stew with Rosemary Croutons

Brined Pork Roast with Chestnut and
Red Cabbage Sauté

Maple Mashed Squash with Candied Pecans

Lima Beans with Ham and Cream

Apple-Cheddar Cornbread

White Chocolate Rice Pudding with
Dried Cherry Sauce

serves 8

menu prep plan

1 day ahead:

- Marinate pork loin in refrigerator.
- Prepare Rosemary Croutons; store at room temperature in airtight container.
- Chop cabbage and mushrooms and dice onion for Chestnut and Red Cabbage Sauté; chill.
- Cook squash and candied pecans for Maple Mashed Squash with Candied Pecans; chill.
- Prepare Dried Cherry Sauce; chill. Toast almonds; store in airtight container.
- Dice bacon, celery, and onion for Oyster Stew; chill.

morning of:

- Prepare Apple-Cheddar Cornbread.
- Prepare White Chocolate Rice Pudding, but do not add topping; cover and chill.
- Assemble Lima Beans with Ham and Cream, but do not bake; cover and chill.

2 hours ahead:

- Bake Brined Pork Roast; keep warm.
- Bake Lima Beans with Ham and Cream; keep warm.
- Reheat mashed squash and complete preparation of Maple Mashed Squash with Candied Pecans.
- Prepare Oyster Stew; keep warm.

30 minutes ahead:

- Cook Chestnut and Red Cabbage Sauté.

last minute:

- Carve Brined Pork Roast.
- Reheat cornbread.
- Spoon rice pudding into serving dishes; top with sauce and almonds.

Brined Pork Roast with Chestnut
and Red Cabbage Sauté, Maple
Mashed Squash with Candied
Pecans, Apple-Cheddar Cornbread,
Lima Beans with Ham and Cream

editor's favorite

Oyster Stew with Rosemary Croutons

Here's a thick, rich, and comforting stew that will warm you up after holiday shopping.

Prep: 12 min.   Cook: 22 min.

2   bacon slices, diced
1   cup finely diced celery
1   cup finely diced onion
½   cup vermouth
2   pints fresh oysters, undrained
2   tablespoons all-purpose flour
2   (8-ounce) bottles clam juice
3   cups half-and-half
1   teaspoon salt
¼   teaspoon pepper
2   teaspoons chopped fresh thyme
2   tablespoons chopped fresh parsley
Rosemary Croutons

Cook first 3 ingredients in a Dutch oven over medium heat 12 minutes or until onion and celery are tender. Add vermouth, and simmer 1 minute. Add oysters.

Whisk together flour and clam juice in a small bowl; whisk into soup. Bring to a simmer over medium heat. Simmer 1 minute or until oyster edges begin to curl. Reduce heat to medium-low; add half-and-half and next 4 ingredients. Cook over medium-low heat until thoroughly heated. (Do not boil.) Serve with Rosemary Croutons. Yield: 10½ cups.

Fix it Faster: Use prechopped fresh celery and onion that's now available in most grocery store produce departments.

Rosemary Croutons

Sprinkle these garlic-and-herb croutons over salads, too.

Prep: 4 min.   Cook: 16 min.

⅓   cup butter or margarine
2   garlic cloves, minced
2   teaspoons chopped fresh rosemary
¼   teaspoon salt
⅛   teaspoon pepper
4   cups (1-inch) French bread cubes

Melt butter in a large nonstick skillet; add garlic and next 3 ingredients. Sauté 1 minute over medium heat. Add bread cubes, tossing gently to coat.

Cook over medium heat, stirring occasionally, 15 minutes or until bread is lightly toasted. Yield: 4 cups.

editor's favorite
Brined Pork Roast with Chestnut and Red Cabbage Sauté

Brining, soaking lean cuts of meat in a solution of water and salt, is a technique used to achieve moist, juicy meat. Our recipe replaces water with apple cider. Mustard, sugar, and molasses are added for flavor.

Prep: 7 min.   Cook: 1 hr., 21 min.   Other: 24 hrs., 10 min.

5   cups apple cider
½   cup firmly packed dark brown sugar
2   tablespoons salt
2   tablespoons prepared mustard
2   tablespoons molasses
2   bay leaves, crumbled
1   (4-pound) boneless pork loin roast
1   tablespoon olive oil
Chestnut and Red Cabbage Sauté

Combine first 6 ingredients, stirring until sugar dissolves. Place pork in a large zip-top freezer bag; add cider mixture. Seal bag, and chill 24 hours.

Remove pork from brine, and pat dry with paper towels; discard brine. Heat oil in a large skillet over medium-high heat; add pork. Cook 6 minutes or until browned on all sides,

turning meat occasionally. Place pork on a rack in a lightly greased shallow roasting pan.

Bake at 300° for 1 hour and 15 minutes or until a meat thermometer inserted into thickest portion registers 150°. Remove from oven; cover and let rest 10 minutes or until thermometer reaches 160° before slicing. Serve with Chestnut and Red Cabbage Sauté. Yield: 8 to 10 servings.

Chestnut and Red Cabbage Sauté

Serve a hefty ¼ cup of this savory accompaniment over each slice of Brined Pork Roast.

Prep: 9 min.   Cook: 17 min.

2   tablespoons butter
1   small onion, diced
1   cup coarsely chopped mushrooms
2   cups coarsely chopped red cabbage
1   cup diced chestnuts from a jar*
2   teaspoons sugar
½   teaspoon salt
1   teaspoon cider vinegar

Melt butter in a large skillet over medium heat; add onion, and sauté 3 minutes or until tender. Add mushrooms; sauté 2 minutes. Add cabbage and chestnuts; sauté 2 minutes. Stir in sugar and salt; cover and simmer 10 minutes or until cabbage is tender. Stir in vinegar. Yield: 2½ cups.

*Look for whole chestnuts sold in jars at Williams-Sonoma or other cook stores.

Whimsical snow globes serve as place card holders and set a casual tone to your table.

Maple Mashed Squash with Candied Pecans

Serve this delectable squash as an alternative to sweet potatoes.

Prep: 19 min. Cook: 37 min.

1   (4-pound) butternut squash
5   tablespoons butter, divided
7   tablespoons maple syrup, divided
1½ teaspoons maple flavoring
1¼ teaspoons salt, divided
1   cup chopped pecans

Microwave squash on HIGH 2 minutes to soften. Cut in half. Peel squash; remove and discard seeds. Cut squash into 1" squares.

Cook squash in water in a large Dutch oven 30 minutes or until tender; drain.

Combine squash, 3 tablespoons butter, 3 tablespoons syrup, maple flavoring, and ¾ teaspoon salt in a large bowl; mash with a potato masher until smooth.

Cook pecans, remaining 2 tablespoons butter, remaining ¼ cup maple syrup, and ½ teaspoon salt in a medium skillet over medium-low heat 7 minutes or until syrup caramelizes and pecans begin to brown; cool in a single layer on a plate.

Sprinkle pecans over squash. Serve warm. Yield: 8 servings.

editor's favorite

Lima Beans with Ham and Cream

Maple-honey ham imparts a smoky sweetness to these baby beans simmered in cream.

Prep: 10 min. Cook: 1 hr.

1   tablespoon butter
2   (10-ounce) packages frozen baby lima beans, thawed
½   pound maple-honey ham, diced (we tested with Boar's Head)
1   cup finely diced onion
1   teaspoon salt
¼   teaspoon freshly ground pepper
⅛   teaspoon ground nutmeg
1   cup whipping cream
¼   to ⅓ cup chicken broth

Butter a 2-quart shallow baking dish, and set aside.

Stir together lima beans and remaining ingredients in a large bowl; spoon into prepared dish.

Bake, covered, at 375° for 30 minutes. Uncover; stir and bake 30 more minutes or until bubbly and browned. Serve

with a slotted spoon, if desired. Beans will thicken as they begin to cool. Yield: 6 to 8 servings.

Apple-Cheddar Cornbread

Tidbits of tangy green apple are a nice surprise that balance the cheese in this crusty cast-iron favorite.

Prep: 13 min. Cook: 28 min.

1   tablespoon butter
1   Granny Smith apple, peeled and diced (1 cup)
1   tablespoon shortening
1½ cups yellow cornmeal
½   cup all-purpose flour
1   tablespoon baking powder
½   teaspoon salt
1½ cups milk
1   large egg, lightly beaten
6   tablespoons butter, melted
1   cup (4 ounces) shredded extra-sharp Cheddar cheese

Heat 1 tablespoon butter in a large skillet over medium-high heat until melted. Add apple, and sauté 3 minutes or until just tender. Remove from heat, and set aside.

Preheat oven to 425°. Heat shortening in a 9" cast-iron skillet in oven 5 minutes.

Meanwhile, stir together cornmeal and next 3 ingredients. Whisk together milk and egg; add to dry ingredients, stirring just until moistened. Stir in 6 tablespoons melted butter. Add sautéed apple and cheese, stirring just until combined.

Pour batter into hot skillet. Bake at 425° for 25 minutes or until golden. Cut into wedges. Yield: 8 servings.

editor's favorite

White Chocolate Rice Pudding with Dried Cherry Sauce

The seeds and pod of a vanilla bean simmer in this rich rice pudding. Be sure to stir it often so it doesn't scorch.

Prep: 10 min. Cook: 45 min. Other: 5 min.

1½ cups hot water
¾   cup medium-grain rice
1   vanilla bean, split lengthwise
½   cup sugar
4   cups half-and-half
¼   teaspoon salt
¾   cup white chocolate morsels
Dried Cherry Sauce
½   cup sliced almonds, toasted

White Chocolate Rice Pudding with Dried Cherry Sauce

Combine water and rice in a large saucepan. Bring to a boil. Cover, reduce heat, and simmer 15 minutes or until liquid is absorbed and rice is tender.

Scrape seeds from vanilla bean into pan. Stir seeds, pod, sugar, half-and-half, and salt into rice. Cook over medium-low heat 30 minutes, stirring often. Remove vanilla bean pod. Add white chocolate morsels, stirring until melted. Let cool 5 minutes. Spoon rice pudding into 8 individual serving dishes. If not serving immediately, cover and chill. When ready to serve, top with Dried Cherry Sauce, and sprinkle with almonds. Yield: 8 servings.

quick & easy

Dried Cherry Sauce

Prep: 6 min.   Cook: 27 min.

½	cup dried cherries or cranberries
2	cups Merlot
¾	cup sugar
1	teaspoon grated orange rind
1	teaspoon grated fresh ginger

Combine all ingredients in a medium saucepan. Bring to a boil; reduce heat, and cook, uncovered, 27 minutes or until sauce coats a spoon and is reduced to 1 cup, stirring occasionally. Cool completely. Yield: 1 cup.

33

Mother-Daughter Holiday Tea

Turkey Finger Sandwiches

PB and J Cutouts

Ginger-Honey Bread

Citrus Curd

Buttery Scones   Pink Princess Spread

Fresh strawberries

Instant Spiced Tea Mix   Pink lemonade

serves 12 to 16

menu prep plan

Up to a month ahead
• Prepare Instant Spiced Tea Mix; store in airtight container.

1 day ahead
• Prepare Turkey Finger Sandwiches; cover with a damp paper towel and then plastic wrap, and chill.
• Grate citrus rinds, and squeeze juices for Citrus Curd; cover and chill.
• Prepare Pink Princess Spread; cover and chill.
• Prepare Citrus Curd; cover and chill.

Morning of
• Bake Ginger-Honey Bread; wrap in plastic wrap once cooled.
• Prepare lemonade.

1 hour ahead
• Bake Buttery Scones.
• Let Pink Princess Spread come to room temperature.
• Prepare PB and J Cutouts.
• Wash strawberries, and arrange on platter.

Last minute
• Boil water for tea; place tea mix in a serving bowl.
• Slice Ginger-Honey Bread; serve with Citrus Curd.

Turkey Finger Sandwiches, Buttery Scones, Pink Princess Spread, Fresh strawberries, Instant Spiced Tea, Pink lemonade

make ahead

Turkey Finger Sandwiches

Garnish half of these dainty sandwiches for the grown-ups at your party, leaving the other half plain for little ones.

Prep: 58 min.

½	pound smoked turkey breast, cut into 1-inch cubes
½	cup unsalted butter, cut into pieces and softened
2	teaspoons honey mustard
1	tablespoon orange marmalade
2	teaspoons lemon juice
¼	cup chopped fresh parsley
3	tablespoons chopped fresh chives
¼	teaspoon salt
1	(24-ounce) package sliced firm white bread (we tested with Pepperidge Farm Hearty White)

Fresh whole chives

¼	cup unsalted butter, softened
¼	cup chopped fresh parsley

Process turkey in a food processor until chopped. Add ½ cup butter and next 3 ingredients; process until almost smooth, stopping to scrape down sides. Transfer turkey spread to a medium bowl. Stir in ¼ cup parsley, 3 tablespoons chives, and salt.

Trim crusts from bread, using a serrated or an electric knife.

Spread about ¼ cup turkey spread on 8 bread slices. Top with remaining 8 bread slices; pressing lightly to adhere. Cut each sandwich into 4 fingers, using a serrated knife or an electric knife.

To garnish, tie a whole chive around each finger sandwich, and knot; or spread cut sides of sandwiches with ¼ cup softened butter, and dip lightly into ¼ cup chopped parsley. Arrange on a serving platter. Yield: 32 finger sandwiches.

Note: You can make sandwiches up to 1 day ahead. Just lay a damp paper towel over sandwiches before covering with plastic wrap. Store in refrigerator.

pb and j cutouts

Using your bread of choice and holiday-shaped cutters, cut shapes from bread. (Discard trimmings, or use to make breadcrumbs.) Make peanut butter and jelly sandwiches. Arrange cutouts on a serving platter (see photo on following page).

PB and J Cutouts will delight the daughters at the tea.

(directions previous page)

editor's favorite · gift idea · make ahead

Ginger-Honey Bread

Prep: 12 min.   Cook: 30 min.

½   cup unsalted butter, softened
½   cup firmly packed light brown sugar
1   large egg
½   cup honey
½   cup light molasses
1¾   cups all-purpose flour
1   tablespoon ground ginger
½   teaspoon baking soda
1   teaspoon ground cinnamon
½   teaspoon ground allspice
¼   teaspoon salt
½   cup hot water

Beat butter and sugar in a large bowl at medium speed with an electric mixer until fluffy. Add egg, honey, and molasses, beating until blended. Combine flour and next 5 ingredients; add to butter mixture alternately with water, beginning and ending with flour mixture. Pour batter into a lightly greased and floured 9" square pan.

Bake at 350° for 30 minutes or until a wooden pick inserted in center comes out clean. Cool completely in pan on a wire rack. Cut into 20 rectangles. Yield: 20 servings.

editor's favorite · gift idea · make ahead

Citrus Curd

A thick-skinned navel orange will yield the best rind for this recipe. Spoon this refreshing curd over Ginger-Honey Bread or fresh fruit.

Prep: 6 min.   Cook: 25 min.

2   cups sugar
1   cup butter
2   tablespoons grated lemon rind (about 3 lemons)
1   tablespoon grated lime rind (about 3 limes)
1   tablespoon grated orange rind (1 large orange)
⅓   cup fresh lemon juice
⅓   cup fresh lime juice
4   large eggs, lightly beaten

Combine first 7 ingredients in a heavy nonaluminum saucepan. Cook, whisking constantly, over medium heat 8 to 10 minutes or until butter melts and sugar dissolves.

Gradually whisk about one-fourth of hot sugar syrup into beaten eggs; add to remaining hot syrup, whisking constantly. Reduce heat to medium-low; cook 12 to 15 minutes, stirring gently, or until curd thickens and coats a spoon; let cool. Cover and chill overnight. Yield: 3½ cups.

Buttery Scones

These crusty scones are best right out of the oven.

Prep: 14 min.   Cook: 21 min.

3½   cups unbleached all-purpose flour
¼   cup sugar
2¼   teaspoons baking powder
¼   teaspoon salt
1   cup cold unsalted butter, cut into pieces
1   cup half-and-half
2   large eggs
1   teaspoon water
1   tablespoon sugar
Pink Princess Spread (optional)

Combine first 4 ingredients in a large bowl; cut in butter with a pastry blender until crumbly.

Whisk together half-and-half and 1 egg in a bowl; add to dry ingredients, stirring with a fork just until dry ingredients are moistened. Turn dough out onto a lightly floured surface, and knead 3 or 4 times.

Divide dough in half; shape each into a ball. Pat each into a 5½" circle on a lightly greased baking sheet. Cut each circle into 6 wedges, using a sharp knife (do not separate wedges).

Whisk together remaining egg with 1 teaspoon water in a small bowl; brush egg wash over dough. Sprinkle 1 tablespoon sugar evenly over dough.

Bake at 425° for 19 to 21 minutes or until golden. Serve warm. Serve with Pink Princess Spread, if desired. Yield: 1 dozen.

Pink Princess Spread

Prep: 8 min.

1   (8-ounce) package cream cheese, softened
¼   cup butter or margarine, softened
2   teaspoons powdered sugar
¼   cup squeezable strawberry spread (we tested with Welch's)

Beat cream cheese, butter, and powdered sugar at medium speed with an electric mixer until smooth. Stir in strawberry spread. Cover and chill. Yield: 1½ cups.

gift idea • make ahead

Instant Spiced Tea Mix

Serve this tea mix in a sugar bowl next to a teapot of boiling water. Make an extra batch, and give small jars of the mix as party favors.

Prep: 5 min.

1   cup lemonade-flavored iced tea (we tested with Country Time)
1   cup orange-flavored breakfast drink mix
1   teaspoon ground cinnamon
½   teaspoon ground cloves
¼   teaspoon ground nutmeg
¼   teaspoon ground ginger

Combine all ingredients in a large zip-top plastic bag.

To make 1 serving, place 2 heaping tablespoons spiced tea mix in a cup; add 1 cup boiling water, and stir gently. Yield: 2 cups mix.

Instant Spiced Tea Mix, Citrus Curd

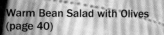
Warm Bean Salad with Olives
(page 40)

Tuscan Dinner Party

Warm Bean Salad with Olives

Chicken with 40 Cloves of Garlic

Herb-Parmesan Smashed Potatoes

Broccoli with Balsamic Butter

Chocolate-Espresso Pots de Crème or

Chocolate Panini

serves 6 to 8

menu prep plan

6 hours ahead:

• Cook cauliflower, dice celery and onion, and mince garlic for Warm Bean Salad with Olives; chill.

• Cut broccoli into florets; chill.

• Prepare Chocolate-Espresso Pots de Crème; cover and chill.

2½ hours ahead:

• Prepare Chicken with 40 Cloves of Garlic for roasting; bake and keep warm.

• Complete preparation of Warm Bean Salad with Olives.

1 hour ahead:

• Prepare Broccoli with Balsamic Butter.

• Microwave potatoes; prepare Herb-Parmesan Smashed Potatoes. Keep warm.

last minute:

• Carve chicken.

just after dinner:

• Prepare Chocolate Panini, or serve Chocolate-Espresso Pots de Crème.

Warm Bean Salad with Olives

Chicken with 40 Cloves of Garlic,
Herb-Parmesan Smashed Potatoes,
Broccoli with Balsamic Butter

Warm Bean Salad with Olives

Prep: 23 min.   Cook: 11 min.

2	cups small fresh cauliflower florets (about 1 [10-ounce] package)
½	cup extra-virgin olive oil, divided
1	cup diced celery
1	cup diced red onion
2	garlic cloves, minced
⅓	cup white wine vinegar
1	tablespoon honey
2	(15.5-ounce) cans cannellini beans, rinsed and drained
1	(7-ounce) jar pitted kalamata olives, halved
2	tablespoons chopped fresh parsley
1	tablespoon chopped fresh sage
1	teaspoon salt
¼	teaspoon freshly ground pepper

Garnish: fresh sage

Cook cauliflower in boiling water to cover 5 to 6 minutes or until crisp-tender. Plunge into ice water to stop the cooking process; drain and set aside.

Heat ¼ cup olive oil in a large skillet over medium-high heat until hot. Add celery and onion; sauté 3 minutes or until almost tender. Add garlic; sauté 30 seconds. Stir in vinegar and honey, stirring to dissolve honey.

Combine cauliflower and sautéed vegetables in a large bowl. Add remaining ¼ cup olive oil, beans, and next 5 ingredients; stir well to combine. Serve warm or at room temperature. Garnish, if desired. Yield: 6 to 8 servings.

Chicken with 40 Cloves of Garlic

Chicken with 40 Cloves of Garlic

The abundance of garlic mellows in flavor during roasting.

Prep: 10 min. Cook: 1 hr., 45 min.

2   (3-pound) whole chickens
8   fresh thyme sprigs
¼   cup butter, softened
1   lemon, halved
2   teaspoons salt
1   teaspoon freshly ground pepper
40 garlic cloves, unpeeled (about 3 bulbs)
1   to 2 tablespoons olive oil
Garnish: fresh thyme

Rinse chickens, and pat dry with paper towels. Place 4 thyme sprigs in cavity of each bird. Rub each chicken with 2 tablespoons softened butter. Squeeze a lemon half over each chicken. Sprinkle with salt and pepper.

Tie ends of legs together with string; tuck wing tips under. Place chickens, breast side up, in a well-greased shallow roasting pan.

Toss garlic with olive oil in a bowl. Scatter garlic cloves around chickens, snuggling them close to chickens.

Bake at 375° for 1 hour and 45 minutes or until a meat thermometer inserted into thigh registers 180°.

Remove chickens and garlic to a serving platter. Garnish, if desired. Yield: 6 to 8 servings.

Herb-Parmesan Smashed Potatoes

This dish can be prepared at the last minute and doesn't take up any space on the cooktop.

Prep: 18 min.   Cook: 15 min.

5	russet potatoes (about 3 pounds)
3	tablespoons butter
½	cup half-and-half
1	cup freshly grated Parmigiano-Reggiano cheese
2	teaspoons chopped fresh rosemary
2	tablespoons chopped fresh flat-leaf parsley
1	teaspoon salt
½	teaspoon freshly ground pepper

Pierce potatoes with a fork. Microwave on HIGH 13 to 15 minutes or until tender; let cool slightly. Peel potatoes; mash with a potato masher. Add butter and remaining ingredients, mashing until blended. Serve warm. Yield: 6 to 8 servings.

Chocolate-Espresso Pots de Crème

Broccoli with Balsamic Butter

Prep: 19 min.   Cook: 14 min.

3	pounds broccoli, cut into large florets
½	cup white balsamic vinegar
¼	cup minced shallot
½	cup cold butter, cut into ½" pieces
1	tablespoon chopped fresh parsley
½	teaspoon salt
⅛	teaspoon pepper

Place broccoli florets in a steamer basket over boiling water, and cook 7 minutes or until crisp-tender.

Meanwhile, in a medium skillet, bring vinegar and shallots to a boil; reduce heat, simmer 7 minutes or until vinegar is almost absorbed. Remove from heat; add butter, a few pieces at a time, stirring constantly with a wire whisk until butter melts and sauce thickens. Stir in parsley, salt, and pepper. Toss with steamed broccoli. Yield: 8 servings.

Fix it Faster: Buy broccoli crowns to save a step in the kitchen.

Chocolate-Espresso Pots de Crème

Using premium chocolate guarantees velvety texture for this decadent dessert. Look for chocolate (below) in specialty grocery stores.

Prep: 10 min.   Cook: 24 min.   Other: 4 hrs.

2	cups half-and-half
½	cup sugar
2	large eggs, lightly beaten
1	tablespoon instant espresso powder
¼	cup unsweetened cocoa
¼	cup brandy
8	ounces semisweet chocolate, cut into chunks (we tested with Scharffen Berger)

Garnishes: unsweetened whipped cream, lavender

Whisk together first 6 ingredients in top of a double boiler; add chocolate. Bring water to a boil. Reduce heat to medium-low; cook, whisking constantly, 24 minutes or until mixture reaches 160° (mixture will be moderately thickened).

Remove from heat. Spoon chocolate into demitasse cups, chocolate pots, or 4- or 6-ounce ramekins. Cover and chill at least 4 hours. Garnish, if desired. Yield: 6 to 8 servings.

Note: Demitasse cups or chocolate pots will yield smaller servings than ramekins, which is a good option for such a rich dessert.

Chocolate Panini

A slender loaf of rustic Italian bread is the ideal shape to use for these little dessert sandwiches. Get your dinner guests involved in making and serving these hot off the press.

Prep: 3 min. Cook: 1 min. per batch

1   (8-ounce) loaf ciabatta bread
2   to 3 tablespoons olive oil
1   (4-ounce) bittersweet chocolate baking bar, coarsely chopped (we tested with Ghirardelli)

Preheat panini press according to manufacturer's instructions.

Slice bread into 10 (1") pieces; slice each piece in half. Brush crust sides of each piece of bread with olive oil. Turn bottoms of bread, oiled side down. Place chocolate evenly on bottom pieces of bread; cover with tops of bread, oiled side up.

Place 5 sandwiches in panini press; cook 1 minute or just until chocolate begins to melt and bread is toasted. Repeat procedure with remaining sandwiches. Serve hot. Yield: 10 sandwiches.

Chocolate Panini

Vegetarian Night

Caramelized Onion and Mushroom Bisque

Black-eyed Pea Cakes with Cranberry-Red Pepper Salsa

Autumn Succotash with Gruyère Grits

Pumpkin-Pecan Layer Cake

serves 6

menu prep plan

2 or 3 days ahead:
- Prepare Cranberry-Red Pepper Salsa; chill.

1 day ahead:
- Make Pumpkin-Pecan Layer Cake; chill overnight.
- Cook onions for Caramelized Onion and Mushroom Bisque up to the point of adding 2 cups broth; chill.
- Cut bell peppers, fennel, and onion for Autumn Succotash; chill.
- Prepare Black-eyed Pea Cakes, but do not cook; chill overnight.

2 hours ahead:
- Slice mushrooms and complete preparation of Caramelized Onion and Mushroom Bisque; keep warm.
- Prepare Autumn Succotash; keep warm.

1 hour ahead:
- Prepare Gruyère Grits; keep warm.
- Fry Black-eyed Pea Cakes; keep warm.

last minute:
- Spoon Cranberry-Red Pepper Salsa into serving dish.
- Ladle Caramelized Onion and Mushroom Bisque into bowls.

Pumpkin-Pecan
Layer Cake

---

editor's favorite

Caramelized Onion and Mushroom Bisque

Prep: 15 min.   Cook: 52 min.   Other: 30 min.

2   tablespoons butter
3   pounds onions, sliced and separated into rings
2   garlic cloves, chopped
4½   cups vegetable broth, divided
2   tablespoons olive oil
4   (3.5-ounce) packages shiitake mushrooms, stems removed and sliced
½   teaspoon salt
½   cup whipping cream
2   tablespoons dry sherry
1   tablespoon fresh lemon juice
¼   teaspoon salt
⅛   teaspoon ground white pepper
Sour cream (optional)

Melt butter in a Dutch oven over medium heat; add onions. Cook over medium heat, stirring occasionally, 35 minutes or until onion is lightly browned and very tender. Add garlic, and cook 1 minute. Add 1 cup broth, stirring to loosen browned bits from bottom of pan (can make ahead to this point. Remove onions from heat; cover and chill until ready to prepare remainder of soup). Stir in 2 cups broth; bring to a boil. Cover, reduce heat, and simmer 10 minutes. Remove from heat, and let cool 30 minutes.

Meanwhile, heat oil in a large skillet over medium-high heat. Add mushrooms, and cook 8 to 10 minutes, stirring once or twice, until mushrooms are lightly browned and liquid has evaporated; stir in ½ teaspoon salt. Remove from heat, and set aside.

Process soup, in batches, in a blender or food processor 2 minutes or until smooth, stopping to scrape down sides. Return to Dutch oven. Stir in remaining 1½ cups broth and whipping cream; bring to a boil. Remove from heat; stir in sherry, lemon juice, ¼ teaspoon salt, and pepper.

To serve, ladle soup into individual bowls, and top evenly with mushrooms; dollop each with sour cream, if desired. Yield: 7 cups.

Make Ahead: To jump-start this recipe, begin a day ahead and caramelize the onions up to the point of adding 2 cups of broth.

Black-eyed Pea Cakes with
Cranberry-Red Pepper Salsa

make ahead

Black-eyed Pea Cakes with Cranberry-Red Pepper Salsa

Here's a knife and fork appetizer with pizzazz; serve two patties as a meatless entrée.

Prep: 27 min.   Cook: 3 min. per batch   Other: 8 hrs.

2   (15.83-ounce) cans black-eyed peas, rinsed and drained
1   large egg
1   teaspoon ground cumin
¾   teaspoon salt
1¼   cups Japanese breadcrumbs (panko), divided
½   cup bottled roasted red peppers, drained and chopped
⅓   cup chopped red onion
⅓   cup chopped fresh cilantro
3   tablespoons all-purpose flour
2   garlic cloves, minced
Peanut oil for frying
Cranberry-Red Pepper Salsa

Process 1½ cups black-eyed peas in a food processor until coarsely chopped.

Whisk together egg, cumin, and salt in a large bowl. Add chopped peas, remaining whole peas, ¾ cup breadcrumbs, and next 5 ingredients; stir well to combine.

Place remaining ½ cup breadcrumbs in a shallow dish.

Using a ¼ cup measure, shape pea mixture into a cake; dredge in breadcrumbs. Repeat with remaining mixture and breadcrumbs. Place cakes on a baking sheet lined with plastic wrap; cover and chill overnight.

Pour oil to a depth of 1" into a large skillet; heat to 350°.

Fry cakes, in batches, 3 minutes or until golden. Drain well on paper towels. Serve immediately with Cranberry-Red Pepper Salsa. Yield: 12 appetizer or 6 entrée servings.

Freezer Note: If you won't be serving all the Black-eyed Pea Cakes at once, freeze uncooked cakes; then thaw before dredging in breadcrumbs and frying.

make ahead · quick & easy

Cranberry-Red Pepper Salsa

This pretty salsa can be made up to three days before serving.

Prep: 15 min.

1½   cups fresh or frozen cranberries, thawed
½   cup bottled roasted red bell peppers, drained and chopped
3   tablespoons honey
½   teaspoon grated lime zest
2   tablespoons lime juice
1   green onion, chopped
1   jalapeño pepper, seeded and minced
2   tablespoons chopped fresh cilantro

Process cranberries in a food processor until coarsely chopped; transfer to a bowl. Add bell peppers and remaining ingredients, stirring well to combine. Cover and chill until ready to serve. Serve cold or at room temperature. Yield: 2 cups.

Autumn Succotash with
Gruyère Grits

editor's favorite

Autumn Succotash with Gruyère Grits

Grits are a versatile base for this rustic blend of corn, onion, garlic, and fennel.

Prep: 18 min.   Cook: 26 min.

2   tablespoons butter or margarine
1   large fennel bulb, cut into thin 2" strips
1   medium onion, cut into ¼" wedges
2   garlic cloves, minced
1   large red bell pepper, cut into thin 2" strips
1   large yellow bell pepper, cut into thin 2" strips
1   (16-ounce) bag frozen whole kernel corn, thawed
1   (10-ounce) package baby lima beans, thawed
½   cup heavy whipping cream
⅓   cup chopped flat-leaf parsley
2   tablespoons fresh lemon juice
1   teaspoon salt
½   teaspoon freshly ground black pepper
Gruyère Grits
4   medium plum tomatoes, chopped (about 1 cup)

Melt butter in a large nonstick skillet over medium heat. Add fennel, onion, and garlic; cook 9 to 11 minutes or until lightly browned, stirring often.

Add peppers; cook 10 minutes, stirring occasionally. Add corn, lima beans, and whipping cream; cook 5 minutes or until thoroughly heated, stirring often. Remove from heat; stir in parsley and next 3 ingredients. Serve over Gruyère Grits. Sprinkle with chopped tomato. Yield: 6 to 8 servings.

Gruyère Grits

Prep: 5 min.   Cook: 15 min.

4   cups vegetable broth
1½ cups uncooked regular grits
1   cup (4 ounces) shredded Gruyère cheese
3   tablespoons butter
½   teaspoon salt
½   teaspoon freshly ground pepper

Bring broth to a boil in a large saucepan. Gradually stir in grits. Cover, reduce heat, and simmer 15 minutes or until tender, stirring occasionally. Remove from heat; stir in cheese and remaining ingredients. Serve immediately. Yield: 6 to 8 servings.

editor's favorite • make ahead

Pumpkin-Pecan Layer Cake

Prep: 30 min.   Cook: 20 min.   Other: 8 hrs., 10 min.

½   cup butter, softened
1½ cups firmly packed light brown sugar
2   large eggs
1   cup canned pumpkin
2   cups all-purpose flour
2   teaspoons baking powder
2   teaspoons pumpkin pie spice
½   teaspoon baking soda
½   teaspoon salt
½   cup buttermilk
2   teaspoons vanilla extract
2   teaspoons minced fresh ginger
1   cup chopped pecans, toasted
Ginger-Cream Cheese Frosting

Beat butter and sugar at medium speed with an electric mixer until light and fluffy. Add eggs, 1 at a time, beating until blended after each addition. Add pumpkin, beating until blended.

Combine flour and next 4 ingredients. Combine buttermilk, vanilla, and ginger. Add flour mixture to butter mixture alternately with gingered buttermilk, beginning and ending with flour mixture. Beat at low speed after each addition. Fold in chopped pecans. Pour batter into 2 greased, parchment paper-lined 9" round cakepans.

Bake at 350° for 18 to 20 minutes or until a wooden pick inserted in center comes out clean. Cool in pans on wire racks 10 minutes; remove from pans, and cool completely on wire racks.

Spread Ginger-Cream Cheese Frosting between layers and on top and sides of cake. Cover and chill overnight. Yield: 1 (2-layer) cake.

Ginger-Cream Cheese Frosting

Prep: 7 min.   Other: 30 min.

1½ (8-ounce) packages cream cheese, softened
½   cup butter, softened
1   tablespoon minced fresh ginger
4   cups powdered sugar
1   teaspoon vanilla extract

Beat first 3 ingredients at medium speed with an electric mixer until light and fluffy. Gradually add powdered sugar, beating until smooth. Add vanilla, beating until smooth. Chill 30 minutes or until spreading consistency. Yield: 2¼ cups.

Brunch Buffet

Hearts of Romaine Salad with
Walnut-Champagne Vinaigrette

Spinach and Gruyère Tarts

Rosemary Biscuits and Fresh Pork Sausage Patties

Ham-and-Hash Brown Breakfast Casserole

Banana Nut and Dulce de Leche Coffee Cake

Tropical Fruit with Ginger Syrup

Berry Fizz   Coffee   Orange juice

serves 12

menu prep plan

2 days ahead:

• Prepare Walnut-Champagne Vinaigrette; chill.

• Make dough for Rosemary Biscuits; freeze unbaked biscuits.

• Chill Champagne.

1 day ahead:

• Wash romaine hearts and trim stems; chill. Toast walnuts for salad.

• Fill tart shells with spinach and cheese; prepare egg mixture for Spinach and Gruyère Tarts. Cover both, and chill overnight.

• Prepare Ham-and-Hash Brown Breakfast Casserole, but do not bake; chill overnight.

• Process all ingredients for Fresh Pork Sausage Patties; chill overnight.

• Bake Banana Nut and Dulce de Leche Coffee Cake; cover and store at room temperature.

• Cut fruit and prepare Ginger Syrup for Tropical Fruit; chill separately. Toast coconut, and store in airtight container.

3 hours ahead:

• Combine cranberry juice and liqueur for Berry Fizz; chill.

1 to 2 hours ahead:

• Bake Ham-and-Hash Brown Breakfast Casserole.

• Cook Fresh Pork Sausage Patties; keep warm.

• Add egg mixture to tart shells, and bake Spinach and Gruyère Tarts.

• Assemble Tropical Fruit with Ginger Syrup.

• Bake frozen biscuits at 425° for 15 minutes; keep warm.

last minute:

• Arrange Hearts of Romaine Salad on serving plates.

• Reheat Banana Nut and Dulce de Leche Coffee Cake.

• Stir Champagne into Berry Fizz.

Tropical Fruit with Ginger Syrup, Banana Nut and Dulce de Leche Coffee Cake, Spinach and Gruyère Tarts, Ham-and-Hash Brown Breakfast Casserole

editor's favorite • make ahead

Hearts of Romaine Salad with Walnut-Champagne Vinaigrette

Prep: 10 min.

⅓   cup champagne vinegar
⅓   cup walnut oil or extra-virgin olive oil
2   tablespoons minced shallot (about 1 large)
2   tablespoons chopped fresh flat-leaf parsley
1   tablespoon chopped fresh thyme
¾   teaspoon salt
½   teaspoon freshly ground pepper
4   romaine hearts*
½   cup chopped walnuts, toasted

Whisk together first 7 ingredients.

Remove lower 3" of romaine stems. Arrange leaves on a large serving platter. Drizzle evenly with Walnut-Champagne Vinaigrette. Sprinkle with walnuts. Yield: 10 to 12 servings.

Make Ahead: You can make Walnut-Champagne Vinaigrette up to 2 days ahead.

*You can find washed, ready-to-serve romaine hearts at most grocery stores.

Spinach and Gruyère Tarts

Prep: 15 min.   Cook: 35 min.   Other: 5 min.

2   (10-ounce) packages frozen tart shells (we tested with Dutch Ann)
1   (10-ounce) package frozen chopped spinach, thawed and squeezed dry
1½ cups (6 ounces) shredded Gruyère cheese
4   large eggs
1½ cups half-and-half
½   teaspoon salt
½   teaspoon freshly ground pepper
Ground nutmeg

Arrange tart shells on a baking sheet. Fill each shell with about 1 tablespoon each spinach and cheese.

Whisk together eggs and next 3 ingredients. Spoon egg mixture evenly into tart shells. Sprinkle lightly with nutmeg.

Bake at 375° for 30 to 35 minutes or until tarts are puffed and crust is lightly browned. Let stand 5 minutes before removing from foil pans. Yield: 16 tarts.

Make Ahead: To make ahead, simply fill the pastry with the spinach and cheese, and prepare the egg mixture. Cover both, and chill overnight. Next day, fill tarts with egg mixture, and bake.

editor's favorite • make ahead

Rosemary Biscuits

Prep: 25 min.   Cook: 10 min.

3   cups self-rising soft-wheat flour
¼   cup sugar
½   teaspoon salt
½   cup shortening, chilled
1   cup buttermilk
½   cup whipping cream
1½ tablespoons chopped fresh rosemary
Fresh Pork Sausage Patties
Garnish: rosemary sprigs

Combine first 3 ingredients in a large bowl. Cut shortening into flour mixture with a pastry blender until mixture resembles coarse meal. Add buttermilk, whipping cream, and rosemary, stirring with a fork until all ingredients are moistened. (Dough with be soft.)

Turn dough out onto a generously floured surface; knead 3 or 4 times. Pat or roll dough to 1" thickness; cut with a floured 2" biscuit cutter, and place biscuits 1" apart on ungreased baking sheets.

Bake at 450° for 10 minutes or until lightly browned. Transfer to a wire rack, and cool slightly. Split biscuits with a fork, and fill with warm Fresh Pork Sausage Patties. Serve hot. Garnish, if desired. Yield: 20 biscuits.

Make Ahead: Make the biscuit dough several days in advance, and freeze unbaked biscuits in a single layer on a baking sheet until frozen solid. Transfer to a large zip-top freezer bag. Seal and store in freezer. Arrange frozen biscuits on an ungreased baking sheet. Bake at 425° for 15 minutes or until golden.

editor's favorite • make ahead

Fresh Pork Sausage Patties

This homemade sausage is best when made in advance, giving it more time to develop flavor. The patties can also be cooked in advance and refrigerated or frozen. Simply reheat them in the microwave when ready to serve.

Prep: 30 min.   Cook: 4 min. per batch   Other: 4 hrs.

6   bacon slices, frozen and coarsely chopped
2   garlic cloves
1   shallot
2   teaspoons fresh rosemary leaves
1½ teaspoons ground sage
¾   teaspoon salt
½   teaspoon freshly ground black pepper
¼   teaspoon ground red pepper
1½ pounds ground pork

Process first 8 ingredients in a food processor until finely minced. Add ground pork; process until mixture begins to form a ball. Cover and chill at least 4 hours or overnight.

Shape sausage into 20 (3 x ¼") patties. Cook in several batches in a large nonstick skillet over medium-high heat 2 minutes per side or until lightly browned and a thermometer inserted into the thickest portion registers 160°. Keep warm until ready to serve. Yield: 20 patties.

Turkey Sausage Patties: You can make this recipe using 1½ pounds ground turkey (white and dark meat). Follow above procedure, except blend ground turkey with seasonings by hand instead of using a processor. This will keep the turkey from becoming too finely ground.

Tropical Fruit with Ginger Syrup, Banana Nut and Dulce de Leche Coffee Cake, Berry Fizz, Rosemary Biscuits and Fresh Pork Sausage Patties

Ham-and-Hash Brown Breakfast Casserole

Make breakfast a breeze by preparing this casserole the day before. Simply spoon potato mixture into a dish, cover, and chill overnight. Next morning, place casserole directly into the oven, and add 15 minutes to the initial bake time.

Prep: 15 min. Cook: 1 hr., 10 min. Other: 10 min.

8	bacon slices
¾	cup chopped sweet onion
⅓	cup butter
1	(30-ounce) package frozen country-style hash brown potatoes, thawed
1	(10¾-ounce) can cream of chicken soup
1	(16-ounce) container sour cream
2	cups (8 ounces) shredded Colby Jack cheese
1	(8-ounce) package diced ham
1	(4-ounce) jar diced pimiento, drained
2	tablespoons coarse-grained Dijon mustard
½	teaspoon salt
½	teaspoon freshly ground pepper

Cook bacon in a large nonstick skillet over medium heat until very crisp. Remove bacon from pan, reserving 2 tablespoons drippings in pan. Crumble bacon; set aside.

Add onion to reserved drippings; cook over medium-high heat 6 minutes or until tender and golden. Reduce heat to medium-low, and swirl in butter until melted; remove pan from heat.

Squeeze excess moisture from potatoes. Stir in potatoes, soup, and remaining ingredients. Spoon into a greased 13" x 9" baking dish.

Bake, covered, at 350° for 45 minutes. Uncover and sprinkle with crumbled bacon. Bake 15 more minutes or until browned on top. Let stand 10 minutes before serving. Yield: 12 servings.

Banana Nut and Dulce de Leche Coffee Cake

While best served warm, this cake can be made a day ahead and reheated.

Prep: 35 min.   Cook: 39 min.

2¾   cups all-purpose flour, divided
1   cup granulated sugar
1½   teaspoons baking powder
½   teaspoon baking soda
½   teaspoon salt
1   cup cold unsalted butter, cut into pieces and divided
2   large eggs
1   cup mashed banana
½   cup sour cream
1   tablespoon vanilla extract
¼   cup firmly packed light brown sugar
1   cup pecan pieces
1   (13.4-ounce) can dulce de leche (we tested with Nestlé)*

Combine 2¼ cups flour and next 4 ingredients in a large bowl. Cut ¾ cup butter into flour mixture with a pastry blender until crumbly. Whisk together eggs and next 3 ingredients; add to flour mixture, stirring just until dry ingredients are moistened.

Spread batter into a greased 13" x 9" pan.

Combine remaining ½ cup flour and brown sugar in a small bowl. Cut remaining ¼ cup butter into flour mixture with pastry blender. Add pecans, pressing streusel mixture between fingers until large clumps form. Sprinkle streusel over batter in pan.

Microwave dulce de leche in a small glass bowl on HIGH 1 minute or until drizzling consistency, stirring once; drizzle over streusel topping.

Bake at 350° for 35 to 38 minutes or until streusel topping begins to brown and center of cake puffs slightly. Cool slightly. Yield: 12 to 16 servings.

*Find dulce de leche in the ethnic section or on the baking aisle of your grocery store.

make ahead

Tropical Fruit with Ginger Syrup

Purchase tropical fruit several days in advance to allow time for ripening to optimal flavor and sweetness. Leave it at room temperature until ripened; then chill until ready to use.

Prep: 30 min.   Cook: 8 min.

¾   cup water
½   cup sugar
5   thin slices peeled fresh ginger
2   tablespoons fresh lime juice
6   kiwifruit, peeled and sliced
3   mangoes, peeled and cubed
3   star fruit, sliced
1   pineapple, peeled, cored, and cubed
½   (3-pound) Caribbean Red papaya, peeled, seeded, and cubed
Sweetened flaked coconut, toasted

Simmer water, sugar, and ginger in a small saucepan 5 minutes. Remove from heat; pour liquid through a wire-mesh strainer into a small bowl, discarding ginger. Stir in lime juice; cover and chill syrup.

Combine kiwifruit and next 4 ingredients in a trifle bowl or large serving bowl. Drizzle cooled syrup over fruit; toss gently. Sprinkle with toasted coconut. Yield: 20 servings.

editor's favorite • make ahead • quick & easy

Berry Fizz

Float a few fresh raspberries in each Champagne flute when serving this holiday alternative to mimosas.

Prep: 5 min.

6   cups cranberry-raspberry juice drink, chilled (we tested with Ocean Spray)
¼   cup Chambord or other raspberry liqueur
1   (750-milliliter) bottle Champagne, chilled
Garnish: fresh raspberries

Stir together juice and liqueur; chill. Stir in Champagne just before serving. Garnish, if desired. Yield: 10 cups.

Country Dinner

Butter Lettuces with Chutney Vinaigrette

Walnut Chicken with Dijon Cream Sauce

Brussels Sprouts with Marmalade Glaze

Cheddar and Green Onion Muffins

Butterscotch Pudding with Bourbon-
Brown Sugar Meringue

Molasses Cigarillos

serves 6

menu prep plan

1 day ahead:

- Prepare Butterscotch Pudding; cover and chill.
- Flatten chicken breasts using meat mallet; chill.
- Wash Brussels sprouts and trim stem ends; chill.

4 to 5 hours ahead:

- Bake Cheddar and Green Onion Muffins.
- Prepare Chutney Vinaigrette; chill. Combine lettuce, celery, cucumber, and raisins for salad; chill.
- Top Butterscotch Pudding with Bourbon-Brown Sugar Meringue.

2 to 3 hours ahead:

- Prepare Molasses Cigarillos.
- Prepare Brussels Sprouts with Marmalade Glaze; keep warm.

1 hour ahead:

- Prepare Walnut Chicken with Dijon Cream Sauce.

last minute:

- Toss Butter Lettuces with Chutney Vinaigrette.
- Reheat muffins.

Walnut Chicken with Dijon Cream Sauce,
Butter Lettuces with Chutney Vinaigrette,
Cheddar and Green Onion Muffins,
Brussels Sprouts with Marmalade Glaze

quick & easy

Butter Lettuces with Chutney Vinaigrette

Using a prepackaged salad blend makes this a super-quick accompaniment with dinner. If you prefer, use 6 cups of torn Boston or Bibb lettuce.

Prep: 11 min.

½	cup mango chutney
2	tablespoons cider vinegar
2½	teaspoons curry powder
1½	teaspoons coarse-grained Dijon mustard
1	teaspoon salt
½	teaspoon pepper
½	cup olive oil
1	(7-ounce) package butter lettuce and radicchio salad blend (we tested with Fresh Express Riviera Salad blend)
2	celery ribs with leaves, thinly sliced diagonally
¾	cup peeled, seeded, and thinly sliced cucumber
½	cup golden raisins

Whisk together first 6 ingredients in a small bowl; gradually whisk in oil until blended.

Combine lettuce, celery, cucumber, and raisins in a salad bowl; toss well. Just before serving, pour desired amount of dressing over salad, and toss well. Refrigerate any remaining dressing for other uses. Yield: 6 servings.

Walnut Chicken with Dijon Cream Sauce

Substitute pecans for walnuts to give this chicken a Southern accent.

Prep: 26 min.   Cook: 24 min.

¼ cup butter or margarine, melted
½ teaspoon garlic powder
½ cup Japanese or fine, dry breadcrumbs (we tested with panko)
¼ cup all-purpose flour
½ cup finely chopped walnuts
¼ cup sesame seeds
1 teaspoon salt
½ teaspoon freshly ground pepper
6 skinned and boned chicken breasts
2 tablespoons butter or margarine, divided
2 tablespoons olive oil, divided
1 cup heavy whipping cream
2 tablespoons Dijon mustard
2 tablespoons dry sherry
¼ teaspoon salt
⅛ teaspoon freshly ground pepper

Combine ¼ cup butter and garlic powder in a small bowl, stirring well; set aside.

Combine breadcrumbs and next 5 ingredients in a shallow dish, stirring well.

Place each chicken breast between 2 sheets of heavy-duty plastic wrap; flatten to ½" thickness using a meat mallet or rolling pin.

Brush both sides of chicken with garlic butter; dredge in breadcrumbs.

Heat 1 tablespoon butter and 1 tablespoon olive oil in a large skillet over medium heat until butter melts. Add 3 chicken breasts; cook 4 to 6 minutes on each side or until lightly browned and done. Transfer to a serving platter; repeat procedure with remaining chicken, butter, and olive oil.

Meanwhile, combine whipping cream and remaining 4 ingredients in a small saucepan; whisk until blended. Bring to a simmer; cook 10 minutes or until mixture thickens slightly and coats the back of a spoon. Serve sauce with chicken. Yield: 6 servings.

Brussels Sprouts with Marmalade Glaze

Fresh Brussels sprouts are best during the winter months. Choose small sprouts that are firm and bright green.

Prep: 10 min.   Cook: 36 min.

2 pounds fresh Brussels sprouts
1 (32-ounce) container chicken broth
2 tablespoons butter or margarine
½ cup minced onion
2 garlic cloves, minced
½ cup orange marmalade
¼ teaspoon salt
¼ teaspoon pepper

Wash Brussels sprouts thoroughly, and remove any discolored leaves. Trim stem ends. Place Brussels sprouts in a large saucepan; add broth. Bring to a boil over medium-high heat; reduce heat, and simmer 5 minutes or until desired tenderness.

Drain Brussels sprouts, reserving 1 cup chicken broth. Melt butter in saucepan; add onion and garlic. Sauté over medium-high heat 2 minutes or until tender. Add reserved broth and marmalade; bring to a simmer. Cook, stirring often, 15 minutes or until glaze reduces and thickens. Add Brussels sprouts, salt, and pepper; toss well until thoroughly heated. Serve warm. Yield: 6 servings.

quick & easy

Cheddar and Green Onion Muffins

Prep: 10 min.   Cook: 22 min.

2 cups all-purpose flour
1 tablespoon baking powder
1 teaspoon salt
¼ teaspoon garlic powder
¼ teaspoon ground red pepper
1 cup (4 ounces) shredded extra-sharp Cheddar cheese
⅓ cup finely chopped green onions
1 large egg, lightly beaten
1 cup milk
⅓ cup butter, melted

Combine first 5 ingredients in a large bowl; stir well. Stir in cheese and green onions. Make a well in center of mixture.

Whisk together egg, milk, and butter; add to dry ingredients, stirring just until moistened. Spoon into lightly greased muffin pans, filling three-fourths full.

Bake at 375° for 22 minutes or until a wooden pick inserted in center comes out clean. Remove from pans immediately, and serve warm. Yield: 1 dozen.

Butterscotch Pudding with Bourbon-Brown Sugar Meringue

If you prefer a subtle molasses flavor, use the lesser amount of molasses in the pudding. For entertaining, serve the pudding with Molasses Cigarillos.

Prep: 12 min.   Cook: 40 min.   Other: 8 hrs.

¼	cup butter
¾	cup firmly packed light brown sugar
2	to 3 tablespoons molasses
2¼	cups milk, divided
1	cup heavy whipping cream
½	vanilla bean
3	egg yolks
3	tablespoons cornstarch
2	teaspoons vanilla extract
¼	teaspoon salt
½	cup firmly packed light brown sugar
1	tablespoon bourbon
2	tablespoons water
3	egg whites
¼	teaspoon cream of tartar

Combine butter, ¾ cup brown sugar, and molasses in a medium saucepan. Cook over medium heat, stirring constantly, 5 minutes or until sugar dissolves.

Combine 1¾ cups milk and whipping cream in a separate saucepan. Split vanilla bean lengthwise. Scrape seeds from vanilla bean into saucepan; stir in bean pod. Bring just to a simmer over medium heat. Remove and discard vanilla bean pod. Slowly whisk milk mixture into sugar mixture.

Whisk together egg yolks, remaining ½ cup milk, cornstarch, vanilla, and salt in a small bowl. Gradually stir about one-fourth of hot mixture into yolk mixture; add yolk mixture to remaining hot mixture, stirring constantly. Cook over medium heat, stirring constantly, 20 minutes or until thickened. Remove from heat; pour into a 1-quart baking dish. Place plastic wrap directly on surface of pudding; chill at least 8 hours.

Combine ½ cup brown sugar, bourbon, and water in a small saucepan. Cook over medium-low heat 7 minutes or until a candy thermometer reaches 235°.

Meanwhile, beat egg whites and cream of tartar at high speed with an electric mixer until stiff peaks form. Gradually drizzle in hot brown sugar syrup, beating at high speed 2 minutes or until thick and glossy. Mound meringue over chilled pudding, forming peaks with the back of a spoon. Broil 8 inches from heat 2 minutes or until meringue is browned. Yield: 6 servings.

Butterscotch Pudding with Bourbon-Brown Sugar Meringue

Molasses Cigarillos

These buttery, crisp cookies are a tasty complement to any pudding or ice cream.

Prep: 23 min.   Cook: 66 min.   Other: 16 min.

¼	cup butter
6	tablespoons light brown sugar
3	tablespoons molasses
1	teaspoon vanilla extract
¾	cup ground pecans
¼	cup all-purpose flour

Combine first 3 ingredients in a small saucepan. Cook over medium-low heat 1 to 2 minutes or until butter melts and sugar dissolves, whisking constantly. Remove from heat. Stir in vanilla.

Combine ground pecans and flour; add to molasses mixture, stirring until blended.

Working in batches, making 2 cookies at a time, drop batter by 1 tablespoonful onto a lightly greased aluminum foil-lined baking sheet (keep remaining batter covered with a damp cloth).

Bake at 350° for 8 minutes or until golden. Let stand 2 minutes (no longer). Working quickly, carefully roll each delicate cookie into a tight cigarette shape. Cool completely on wire racks. Serve within 3 hours. Yield: 16 cookies.

Ham Dinner

Shrimp and Benne Seed Tartlets

Baked Ham with Mustard-Peach Glaze

Fennel, Apple, and Celery Slaw

Sweet Potato Salad with Bacon Vinaigrette

Bakery rolls

Dark Chocolate Layer Cake

serves 8

menu prep plan

1 day ahead:
• Make and bake tart shells; store in an airtight container.
• Peel and devein shrimp; chill.

morning of:
• Prepare White Chocolate Frosting; chill.
• Bake and assemble Dark Chocolate Layer Cake.
• Bake sweet potato and onion, toast pecans, and prepare Bacon Vinaigrette.
• Cook shrimp, and make shrimp salad; chill.

3 hours ahead:
• Prepare Baked Ham with Mustard-Peach Glaze; keep warm.
• Prepare Fennel, Apple, and Celery Slaw; chill.

1 hour ahead:
• Complete preparation of Sweet Potato Salad with Bacon Vinaigrette.
• Prepare peach nectar sauce for ham.
• Carve ham, and place on serving platter; keep warm.

last minute:
• Assemble Shrimp and Benne Seed Tartlets.
• Heat rolls.

Shrimp and Benne Seed Tartlets

Prep: 17 min.   Cook: 8 min.

Tartlet Shells
1   pound unpeeled, medium-size fresh shrimp
3   cups water
¼   cup mayonnaise
¼   cup sour cream
1   tablespoon grated lemon zest
2   teaspoons fresh lemon juice
2   teaspoons Creole seasoning
⅓   cup diced celery
2   tablespoons thinly sliced green onions
Garnish: thinly sliced green onions

Prepare and bake Tartlet Shells.

Peel and devein shrimp. Bring water to a boil; add shrimp. Cook 3 to 5 minutes or until shrimp turn pink; drain. Coarsely chop shrimp, and pat dry with a paper towel.

Stir together mayonnaise and next 4 ingredients in a large bowl. Add shrimp, celery, and 2 tablespoons green onions.

Fill each Tartlet Shell with 1 heaping tablespoonful shrimp salad. Garnish, if desired. Serve immediately. Yield: 2 dozen.

Make Ahead: Tartlet shells can be baked up to 24 hours ahead. Store in an airtight container.

Tartlet Shells

Prep: 6 min.   Cook: 10 min.   Other: 35 min.

1   cup all-purpose flour
¾   teaspoon salt
5   tablespoons cold butter, cut into pieces
2   tablespoons sesame seeds
1   to 2 tablespoons cold water
½   teaspoon cider vinegar

Place flour and salt in a food processor; pulse until blended. Add butter and sesame seeds; pulse until blended. With processor running, add 1 tablespoon water and vinegar; process until mixture forms a ball, adding more water, if needed. Shape dough into a log; cover and chill 30 minutes.

Place 1½ teaspoons of dough into each ungreased miniature (1¾") muffin cup, pressing gently up sides of cup. Prick sides and bottom of dough with a fork. Bake at 400° for 10 minutes or until edges are lightly browned. Cool in pan on wire racks 5 minutes. Remove from pans, and cool completely on wire rack. Yield: 2 dozen.

Baked Ham with Mustard-Peach Glaze;
Fennel, Apple, and Celery Slaw; bakery roll;
Sweet Potato Salad with Bacon Vinaigrette

Baked Ham with
Mustard-Peach
Glaze

Small and shapely Seckel pears with
stems make a striking garnish.

editor's favorite

Baked Ham with Mustard-Peach Glaze

Basting this ham with peach preserves and mustard creates a glistening entrée that tastes as good as it looks.

Prep: 13 min.   Cook: 2 hrs., 20 min.   Other: 15 min.

1   (8-pound) fully cooked shank portion
     hardwood-smoked ham
1   cup peach preserves
1   (7.3-ounce) jar coarse-grained Dijon mustard
     (we tested with Maille)
2   cups peach nectar, divided
Garnish: Seckel pears

Remove and discard skin from ham. Using a boning knife, score fat on ham ⅛" deep in a diamond pattern. Place ham, fat side up, on a lightly greased rack in a shallow roasting pan. Insert a meat thermometer, making sure it does not touch fat or bone.

Stir together preserves, mustard, and 1 cup peach nectar in a large bowl; pour over ham.

Bake ham, uncovered, at 350° for 2 hours and 20 minutes or until meat thermometer registers 140°, basting with pan juices every 20 minutes.

Transfer ham to a serving platter. Let stand 15 minutes before carving.

Pour pan drippings into a large saucepan. Add remaining 1 cup peach nectar; bring to a boil. Serve sauce with ham. Garnish, if desired. Yield: 8 to 10 servings.

make ahead

Fennel, Apple, and Celery Slaw

Fennel has a delicate licorice flavor and adds a pleasant note in this tangy slaw with apples.

Prep: 27 min.   Other: 4 hrs.

1   tablespoon cider vinegar
1   tablespoon molasses
1   teaspoon Dijon mustard
½   teaspoon salt
¼   teaspoon freshly ground pepper
¼   cup olive oil
1   large fennel bulb
2   unpeeled Granny Smith apples, julienned
2   unpeeled Gala apples, julienned
2   celery ribs, thinly sliced

Whisk together first 5 ingredients in a large bowl; slowly pour in oil, whisking constantly.

Rinse fennel. Trim stalks to within 1" of end. Discard hard outside stalks. Remove tough core from bottom of bulb. Starting at 1 side, cut bulb vertically into thin shreds.

Add fennel, apple, and celery to dressing, tossing to combine. Cover and chill up to 4 hours. Toss well just before serving. Yield: 8 servings.

Sweet Potato Salad with Bacon Vinaigrette

With a nutty, sweet, and roasted flavor, this salad is the ideal side for baked ham.

Prep: 26 min.   Cook: 35 min.

4   pounds sweet potatoes, peeled and cut into
       ¾" pieces
1   small red onion, cut into thin wedges
6   tablespoons olive oil, divided
1½   teaspoons salt, divided
4   thick-cut bacon slices
1   tablespoon cider vinegar
2   teaspoons Dijon mustard
½   teaspoon freshly ground pepper
¾   cup pecan pieces, toasted
½   cup golden raisins

Combine sweet potato, onion, 2 tablespoons olive oil, and ¾ teaspoon salt in a large bowl; toss to coat. Arrange vegetables in a single layer on 2 lightly greased baking sheets.

Bake at 450° for 35 minutes or until browned, removing onion after 25 minutes, and stirring sweet potato.

Meanwhile, cook bacon in a large nonstick skillet over medium heat 12 minutes or until crisp. Drain bacon, reserving 2 tablespoons drippings in pan.

Add remaining ¼ cup olive oil, remaining ¾ teaspoon salt, vinegar, mustard, and pepper to drippings in skillet. Stir well. Transfer vinaigrette to a large bowl. Add roasted sweet potato, onion, pecans, and raisins, tossing gently to coat. Cool. Yield: 8 servings.

Note: If you have only one oven, place 1 baking sheet on the lower oven rack and 1 on the upper rack; switch positions after 25 minutes. Bake 5 to 10 more minutes or until potatoes are browned.

Dark Chocolate Layer Cake

A cake to please all chocolate lovers—dark chocolate layers under a blanket of creamy white chocolate frosting.

Prep: 37 min.   Cook: 22 min.   Other: 10 min.

1	cup butter, softened
¾	cup granulated sugar
¾	cup firmly packed dark brown sugar
2	large eggs
2	ounces sweet dark chocolate, melted and cooled
1	tablespoon vanilla extract
2	cups all-purpose flour
½	cup unsweetened cocoa powder
1½	teaspoons baking soda
¼	teaspoon salt
1½	cups buttermilk

White Chocolate Frosting

Beat butter and sugars at medium speed with an electric mixer until fluffy. Add eggs, 1 at a time, beating until blended after each addition. Add cooled chocolate and vanilla, beating until blended.

Combine flour and next 3 ingredients; add to butter mixture alternately with buttermilk, beginning and ending with flour mixture. Beat at low speed after each addition. Pour batter into 2 greased parchment paper-lined 9" round cakepans.

Bake at 350° for 22 minutes or until a wooden pick inserted in center comes out clean. Cool in pans on wire racks 10 minutes; remove from pans, and cool completely on wire racks.

Spread White Chocolate Frosting between layers and on top and sides of cake. Yield: 1 (2-layer) cake.

White Chocolate Frosting

Prep: 8 min.   Other: 45 min.

1½	(8-ounce) packages cream cheese, softened
½	cup butter, softened
2	(4-ounce) white chocolate baking bars, melted and cooled (we tested with Ghirardelli)
1½	cups powdered sugar
2	teaspoons vanilla extract
2	teaspoons fresh lemon juice

Beat cream cheese and butter at medium speed with an electric mixer until fluffy. Add cooled chocolate, beating until blended. Gradually add powdered sugar, beating until smooth. Add vanilla and lemon juice, beating until blended. Cover and chill 45 minutes or until spreading consistency. Yield: 3½ cups.

Office Party

Take one of these savory or sweet holiday offerings to your next office party, or surprise your coworkers and make all of them. All the recipes have make-ahead merit.

Pomegranate Margaritas

Easy Mushroom Puffs

Scallop Ceviche   Taro chips

Beef and Blue Sandwiches with Caramelized Onions

Asian Chicken Won Ton Cups

Bittersweet Chocolate Fondue

Gingerbread Petits Fours   Pumpkin Pie Truffles

serves 20 to 24

menu prep plan

Up to 1 week ahead:
• Prepare Pumpkin Pie Truffles; chill.

1 day ahead:
• Prepare Gingerbread Petit Fours; store in airtight container in refrigerator.
• Combine ingredients for Pomegranate Margaritas; freeze.
• Prepare sandwich ingredients; bake rolls and store in airtight container, caramelize onions and chill, and make cheese spread and chill.
• Prepare filling for Easy Mushroom Puffs; chill.
• Prepare Scallop Ceviche; chill.
• Prepare chicken mixture, cabbage, and won ton cups for Asian Chicken Won Ton Cups; chill chicken mixture and cabbage separately, and store cups in airtight bag at room temperature.

3 hours ahead:
• Prepare and bake Easy Mushroom Puffs; store in airtight container.

2 hours ahead:
• Reheat onions in microwave; assemble Beef and Blue Sandwiches with Caramelized Onions.
• Arrange fruit and other dippers on platter for Bittersweet Chocolate Fondue.

last minute:
• Prepare rims of Margarita glasses.
• Assemble Asian Chicken Won Ton Cups.
• Arrange Scallop Ceviche and taro chips in serving dishes.
• Microwave Bittersweet Chocolate Fondue; keep warm.

Pomegranate Margaritas

editor's favorite • make ahead

Pomegranate Margaritas

Pomegranate and cranberry juices mingle to make this slushy drink a crowd-pleaser.

Prep: 9 min.   Other: 24 hrs.

6   cups white tequila
12   cups water
4   cups cranberry juice cocktail
2   cups pomegranate juice (we tested with POM)*
1½   cups Triple Sec
2   (10-ounce) cans frozen margarita mix, thawed
2   (11.5-ounce) cans frozen cranberry juice cocktail, thawed and undiluted
2   (12-ounce) cans frozen limeade concentrate, thawed and undiluted
Light corn syrup
Coarse sparkling sugar

Combine first 8 ingredients in a very large plastic container. Cover and freeze at least 24 hours or until slushy.

Pour a small amount of corn syrup onto a flat plate. Pour coarse sugar onto another plate. Dip rims of margarita glasses in corn syrup; dip each glass into sugar. Pour margaritas into prepared glasses. Yield: about 32 cups.

Freezer Note: For more convenient storage, divide Pomegranate Margaritas among zip-top freezer bags.

*Find pomegranate juice year-round in the produce section of your local grocery store.

Easy Mushroom Puffs

Simple ingredients come together in a quick and delicious appetizer that will have everyone asking for the recipe.

Prep: 32 min.   Cook: 15 min. per batch   Other: 1 hr.

1   (8-ounce) container garlic-and-herb cream cheese (we tested with Philadelphia Swirls)
2   (4.5-ounce) jars sliced mushrooms, drained
½   cup chopped onion
¼   cup grated Parmesan cheese
1   teaspoon dried chives
¼   teaspoon hot sauce
1   (17.3-ounce) package frozen puff pastry sheets, thawed
1   large egg
1   tablespoon water
Freshly ground pepper (optional)

Combine first 6 ingredients in a medium bowl; cover and chill 1 hour.

Roll 1 sheet puff pastry into a 16" x 10" rectangle. Cut pastry in half lengthwise. Spread one-fourth of filling (about ½ cup) down center of each rectangle. Whisk together egg and water, and brush edges of pastry with egg wash. Fold pastry in half lengthwise over filling; seal edges of pastry with a fork. Cut each pastry into 10 pieces, and place on a parchment-lined baking sheet.

Repeat procedure with remaining sheet puff pastry and filling. Brush remaining egg wash over top of pastries and, if desired, sprinkle with pepper.

Bake at 400° for 15 minutes or until lightly browned. Yield: 40 puffs.

Make Ahead: Filling can be made up to 2 days ahead and chilled.

make ahead
Scallop Ceviche

Ceviche typically consists of raw fish marinated in citrus juices, which "cook" the fish. We chose to sear our scallops for color and flavor. Find taro (a potatolike root) chips in the organic section or the chip aisle of your grocer.

Prep: 20 min.   Cook: 2 min. per batch   Other: 4 hrs., 15 min.

1   pound sea scallops
1   teaspoon ground cumin
½   teaspoon salt
2   plum tomatoes, finely chopped
½   cup finely chopped red onion
½   cup finely chopped yellow bell pepper
¼   cup chopped fresh cilantro
½   cup fresh lime juice
1   jalapeño pepper, seeded and minced
¼   teaspoon black pepper

Pat scallops dry; sprinkle with cumin and salt.

Heat a large skillet over high heat. Add scallops, and cook, in 2 batches, 1 minute on each side or until browned. Remove from heat, and let cool 15 minutes. Finely chop scallops, and place in a bowl. Stir in tomato and next 6 ingredients. Cover and chill at least 4 hours or up to 24 hours. Serve with taro chips. Yield: 4 cups.

Beef and Blue Sandwiches with Caramelized Onions

(pictured on following page)

Prep: 27 min.   Cook: 17 min.

2   (25-ounce) packages frozen roll dough (we tested with Rich's)
Blue Cheese Spread (on following page)
1½   pounds premium sandwich-sliced deli roast beef (we tested with Boar's Head)
Caramelized Onions (on following page)

Prepare rolls, and bake according to package directions; cool completely.

Slice rolls in half; spread tops and bottoms of rolls with Blue Cheese Spread. Place roast beef on bottoms of rolls; top beef with Caramelized Onions. Cover with tops. Yield: 4 dozen rolls.

Make Ahead: Rolls, Blue Cheese Spread, and Caramelized Onions can be made a day ahead. Assemble sandwiches no more than 2 hours before serving.

Beef and Blue Sandwiches with Caramelized Onions

Blue Cheese Spread

Choose your "blues." Make your selection from blue-veined cheeses that range in flavor from mildest Maytag, to medium Gorgonzola, to strongest Stilton.

Prep: 7 min.   Other: 2 hrs.

1½   (8-ounce) packages cream cheese, softened
1   (8-ounce) container sour cream
2   teaspoons Worcestershire sauce
1   teaspoon hot sauce
6   ounces blue cheese, crumbled (we tested with Danish blue cheese)
½   cup walnut halves, toasted and chopped

Beat cream cheese at medium speed with an electric mixer until creamy. Add sour cream, Worcestershire sauce, and hot sauce; stir until blended. Stir in blue cheese and walnuts. Cover and chill at least 2 hours. Yield: 3 cups.

Note about Leftovers: Spoon extra spread over steak, or add a splash of milk to transform it into salad dressing.

Caramelized Onions

Prep: 8 min.   Cook: 30 min.

3   tablespoons olive oil
3   large sweet onions, thinly sliced
1½   tablespoons balsamic vinegar
¼   teaspoon freshly ground pepper

Heat oil in a Dutch oven over medium heat; add onions. Cook, stirring often, 30 minutes or until caramelized. Stir in vinegar and pepper. Remove from heat; cool slightly. Yield: 1½ cups.

Asian Chicken Won Ton Cups

Prep: 24 min.   Cook: 14 min.

Vegetable cooking spray
24   won ton wrappers (we tested with Frieda's Asian Specialties)
3   tablespoons creamy peanut butter
3   tablespoons water
2   tablespoons fresh lime juice
1   tablespoon rice wine vinegar
1   tablespoon honey
2   teaspoons chili sauce with garlic (we tested with Hokan)
2   teaspoons dark sesame oil
½   cup sliced almonds, toasted
2   green onions, sliced
1   cup chopped cooked chicken
½   cup shredded napa cabbage

Coat 24 miniature muffin cups with cooking spray. Carefully press 1 won ton wrapper into each muffin cup; spray lightly with cooking spray (wrapper will extend above rim). Bake at 375° for 8 to 10 minutes or until lightly browned and crisp. Remove from pan; cool completely on a wire rack. Store in airtight container until ready to assemble cups.

Meanwhile, whisk together peanut butter and next 6 ingredients. Add sliced almonds, sliced green onions, and chicken; toss to coat. Cover and chill chicken until ready to assemble cups.

Fill won ton cups evenly with cabbage (about 1 teaspoon) and chicken mixture (about 2½ teaspoons) just before serving. Yield: 2 dozen.

Make Ahead: Won ton cups can be baked a day ahead and stored in an airtight container. Chicken filling and cabbage can be prepared a day ahead and chilled separately.

Bittersweet Chocolate Fondue

Arrange fresh strawberries, cubed pineapple, and pear slices on a serving platter as healthy dippers. For more decadent dippers, serve pretzel rods, large marshmallows, biscotti, or cream-filled chocolate sandwich cookies.

Prep: 2 min.   Cook: 2 min.

1   (11.5-ounce) package double chocolate chips
    (we tested with Ghirardelli) or 3 (4-ounce) bars
    bittersweet or dark sweet chocolate
1½ cups whipping cream
2   teaspoons vanilla extract

Combine all ingredients in a microwave-safe bowl; microwave on HIGH for 1½ to 2 minutes, stirring once. Let stand 2 minutes. Stir with a wire whisk until smooth. Keep warm in a fondue pot. Yield: 3 cups.

make ahead

Gingerbread Petits Fours

Traditional petits fours take a holiday turn with home-made gingerbread, spiced cream cheese filling, and a finishing drench in cream cheese frosting.

Prep: 47 min.   Cook: 42 min.   Other: 8 hrs., 10 min

1½ cups all-purpose flour
½   teaspoon baking soda
1½ teaspoons ground ginger
½   teaspoon ground cinnamon
½   teaspoon ground allspice
½   cup butter or margarine, softened
½   cup firmly packed dark brown sugar
1   large egg
½   cup light molasses
1   tablespoon grated fresh ginger
½   cup buttermilk
½   (8-ounce) package cream cheese, softened
¼   cup powdered sugar
⅛   teaspoon ground ginger
1   pinch of ground cinnamon
1   pinch of ground allspice
2   (16-ounce) containers ready-to-spread cream cheese
    frosting (we tested with Duncan Hines)

Whisk together first 5 ingredients in a bowl; set aside.
Beat butter and brown sugar in a large bowl at medium-high speed with an electric mixer until creamy. Add egg; beat until blended. Add molasses and grated ginger; beat until well

blended. Add flour mixture and buttermilk alternately, beginning and ending with dry ingredients. Spread batter into a greased and floured 8" pan.

Bake at 350° for 40 to 42 minutes or until a wooden pick inserted in center comes out clean. Cool in pan on a wire rack 10 minutes. Carefully transfer cake to cooling rack; cool completely. Wrap cake in plastic wrap; chill 8 hours or overnight.

Beat cream cheese and powdered sugar at medium speed until fluffy. Stir in ⅛ teaspoon ginger, pinch of cinnamon, and pinch of allspice. Cut cake in half horizontally, making 2 equal layers. Spread frosting evenly over bottom cake layer. Carefully place remaining cake layer on frosting. Cut cake into 25 squares, using a serrated or an electric knife. Place squares on a rack over a baking sheet.

Remove foil cover from frosting containers. Microwave frosting at HIGH 30 seconds or until melted, stirring once. Pour or spoon frosting over petits fours, coating top and sides completely. If additional frosting is needed, scrape excess frosting from baking sheet and return to container, and microwave on HIGH 15 seconds or until melted. Place petits fours in large candy cups, if desired. Store in an airtight container in refrigerator. Yield: 25 petits fours.

make ahead

Pumpkin Pie Truffles

Prep: 30 min.   Cook: 1 min.   Other: 6 hrs.

1   cup chopped pecans
1   tablespoon butter
2   (4-ounce) white chocolate baking bars, chopped
2   tablespoons butter
¼   cup canned unsweetened pumpkin
½   cup powdered sugar
½   teaspoon ground cinnamon
½   teaspoon vanilla extract
¼   teaspoon ground ginger
⅛   teaspoon salt
9   gingersnaps, coarsely crushed (we tested with Nabisco)

Sauté pecans in 1 tablespoon butter in a large nonstick skillet over medium heat until toasted. Cool completely. Pulse pecans in a food processor until finely chopped.

Combine chocolate and 2 tablespoons butter in a glass bowl. Microwave on HIGH 1 minute; stir until smooth. Stir in pumpkin, next 5 ingredients, and ½ cup pecans. Chill 3 hours or until almost firm.

Combine remaining ½ cup pecans and crushed gingersnaps in shallow dish. Shape pumpkin mixture into 1" balls; roll in pecan mixture. Cover and chill at least 3 hours. Store in refrigerator up to 1 week. Yield: 2½ dozen.

Season's Best Recipes

Find everything you need for the most delicious Christmas season—a stellar casserole collection, slow-cooker holiday favorites, and plenty of gourmet treats that come from your pantry.

Our Best Casseroles

Here's a casserole collection that boasts a variety of big flavors. Each recipe yields enough for a crowd.

Gumbo Casserole with Creamed Garlic Shrimp

A rich brown roux and the signature Cajun culinary trinity (onion, bell pepper, and celery) provide authentic flavors for this hearty dish. It's best served hot from the oven. Call ahead and ask your fishmonger to peel and devein the shrimp for you. (pictured at left)

Prep: 40 min.   Cook: 1 hr., 22 min.

2   pounds unpeeled, medium-size fresh shrimp
1   tablespoon Creole seasoning (we tested with Tony Chachere's)
2   tablespoons bacon drippings
3   tablespoons all-purpose flour
1   tablespoon vegetable oil
⅓   cup finely chopped onion
⅓   cup finely chopped green bell pepper
⅓   cup finely chopped celery
2   garlic cloves, minced
1   teaspoon dried thyme
1   teaspoon dried oregano
¾   teaspoon salt
½   teaspoon pepper
4   green onions, chopped
½   cup chicken broth or water
2   cups whipping cream
1   pound uncooked spaghetti, broken in half and cooked according to package directions
1   cup freshly grated Parmesan cheese
Garnish: additional chopped green onions

Peel and devein shrimp, if desired. Combine shrimp and Creole seasoning in a medium bowl; set aside.

Cook bacon drippings, flour, and oil in a large skillet over medium heat, whisking constantly, 20 to 25 minutes or until roux is the dark brown color of pecan shells. Add ⅓ cup onion and next 3 ingredients; cook 5 minutes or until tender. Add thyme and next 3 ingredients; cook 1 minute, stirring constantly. Add shrimp and 4 green onions; cook over medium-high heat 3 minutes or until shrimp are almost done; transfer to a large bowl.

Add broth to skillet, scraping bottom of skillet to loosen browned bits. Add whipping cream. Bring to a boil over medium-high heat; reduce heat, and simmer 6 minutes. Add to shrimp. Stir in cooked pasta; toss well to combine. Pour into a lightly greased 13" x 9" baking dish. Sprinkle with Parmesan cheese.

Bake, uncovered, at 350° for 20 minutes or until thoroughly heated. Garnish, if desired. Yield: 8 servings.

Deep-Dish Spanakopita

This Greek-flavored casserole starts out on the lowest oven rack to crisp the bottom pastry layer and finishes on the middle rack to ensure a flaky top.

Prep: 44 min.   Cook: 56 min.

2   tablespoons olive oil
8   green onions, chopped (1 cup)
3   garlic cloves, minced
3   (6-ounce) packages fresh baby spinach or 11 cups chopped Swiss chard
¼   cup water
1   (8-ounce) package feta cheese, crumbled
½   cup freshly grated Parmesan cheese
¼   cup chopped dried tomatoes in oil
1   teaspoon dried oregano
¾   teaspoon salt, divided
¼   teaspoon pepper
½   (16-ounce) package frozen phyllo pastry, thawed (we tested with Athens)
⅓   cup butter, melted
1   tablespoon butter
1   tablespoon all-purpose flour
1   cup milk
2   ounces cream cheese, cubed and softened

Heat olive oil in a Dutch oven over medium-high heat until hot. Add green onions and garlic; sauté 3 minutes or until tender. Add spinach and water; cover and cook 8 minutes or until spinach wilts. Cool spinach completely in a colander set over a bowl. Return cooled spinach to pan. Add cheeses, tomatoes, oregano, ½ teaspoon salt, and pepper, stirring well to combine.

Trim phyllo sheets to 13" x 9", if necessary. Layer 8 sheets of phyllo in a lightly greased 13" x 9" baking dish, using half of melted butter to brush between sheets. (Keep remaining phyllo covered with a damp cloth.) Bake at 400° on lowest oven rack for 6 minutes or until lightly browned; set aside.

Melt 1 tablespoon butter in a small saucepan over medium heat. Stir in flour; cook 1 minute. Gradually whisk in milk. Cook over medium heat 2 minutes, whisking constantly. Whisk in cream cheese and remaining ¼ teaspoon salt.

Spread spinach filling over baked phyllo crust; drizzle with white sauce.

Layer remaining phyllo sheets over filling using remaining half of melted butter to brush between sheets. Using a sharp knife, score top layer of phyllo into 8 portions. Bake at 400° on middle oven rack 30 minutes or until pastry is golden. Serve hot. Yield: 8 servings.

Roasted Vegetable Lasagna

This white-sauced meatless lasagna will appeal to a vegetarian crowd.

Prep: 34 min.   Cook: 1 hr., 44 min.   Other: 15 min.

1	medium butternut squash (about 2 pounds)
½	large sweet potato, cut into ½" cubes (about 1 cup)
3	tablespoons olive oil, divided
3	cups sliced leeks (about 5 medium)
1	red bell pepper, cut into thin strips
4	cups milk
4	garlic cloves, halved
3	tablespoons butter or margarine
¼	cup all-purpose flour
1	teaspoon salt
½	teaspoon pepper
9	dried precooked lasagna noodles
1	cup grated Asiago cheese
1	cup whipping cream
½	cup grated Parmesan cheese

Microwave butternut squash at HIGH 2 minutes (This step softens squash for slicing). Cut squash in half lengthwise; remove and discard seeds. Peel squash, and cut into ½" cubes. Set aside 3 cups cubed squash; reserve any remaining squash for another use.

Combine 3 cups squash, sweet potato, and 2 tablespoons olive oil on a large rimmed baking sheet. Bake at 450° for 10 minutes.

Meanwhile, combine leeks, bell pepper, and remaining 1 tablespoon oil in a large bowl. Add to partially roasted squash mixture, stirring gently. Bake at 450° for 20 minutes or until vegetables are tender, stirring after 15 minutes. Return roasted vegetables to bowl; set aside.

Combine milk and garlic in a large saucepan; bring just to a boil. Reduce heat, and simmer, uncovered, 10 minutes. Remove and discard garlic.

Melt butter in a large saucepan over medium heat; whisk in flour until smooth. Cook 1 minute, whisking constantly. Gradually whisk in warm milk; cook over medium-high heat, whisking constantly, 12 to 13 minutes or until slightly thickened. Remove from heat; stir in salt and pepper. Add to roasted vegetables, stirring gently.

Spoon 1 cup vegetable mixture into a lightly greased 13" x 9" baking dish. Top with 3 lasagna noodles; spread half of remaining vegetable mixture over noodles, and sprinkle with ½ cup Asiago cheese. Repeat procedure with 3 noodles, remaining vegetable mixture, and remaining Asiago cheese. Break remaining 3 noodles in half and lay on top of casserole. (Breaking the noodles keeps them from curling up.)

Beat cream at high speed with an electric mixer until soft peaks form. Spread whipped cream over noodles; sprinkle with Parmesan cheese. Bake, covered, at 350° for 30 minutes. Uncover and bake 13 more minutes or until golden and bubbly. Let stand 15 minutes before serving. Yield: 8 servings.

editor's favorite • make ahead

Pizza Strata

As this casserole bakes, the aroma will make you think you've ordered out for pizza. (pictured on page 67)

Prep: 21 min.   Cook: 1 hr.   Other: 16 hrs., 10 min.

1	(16-ounce) French or Italian bread loaf, cut into ½" cubes (about 20 cups)
1	cup finely chopped prosciutto (about 4 ounces)
¼	cup chopped roasted red bell pepper
¼	cup chopped green onions
½	cup freshly grated Parmesan cheese
1	(14½-ounce) can diced tomatoes, undrained
1	cup coarsely chopped pimiento-stuffed olives
1	cup (4 ounces) shredded mozzarella cheese
6	large eggs
3	cups milk
1	teaspoon dried Italian seasoning
½	teaspoon salt
½	teaspoon pepper
¼	cup chopped fresh flat-leaf parsley

Arrange bread cubes in a single layer on large baking sheets. Let stand 8 hours to dry.

Spread half of bread cubes in a lightly greased 13" x 9" baking dish. Sprinkle prosciutto and next 3 ingredients evenly over bread cubes. Arrange remaining bread cubes evenly over Parmesan. Top with tomatoes, olives, and mozzarella cheese.

Whisk together eggs and remaining 5 ingredients. Pour egg mixture evenly over bread cubes, pressing down cubes gently to absorb liquid; cover and chill 8 hours.

Bake, uncovered, at 325° for 55 minutes or until set and top is browned. Let stand 10 minutes before serving. Yield: 8 to 10 servings.

editor's favorite

Chic Mac and Cheese

Blue cheese rules in this pasta classic. Serve it alongside a grilled steak.

Prep: 35 min.   Cook: 1 hr., 5 min.   Other: 5 min.

2	tablespoons butter or margarine
1	large green bell pepper, chopped
1	large red bell pepper, chopped
1	large yellow bell pepper, chopped
4	celery ribs, finely chopped
¼	teaspoon salt
½	cup butter or margarine
½	cup all-purpose flour
2	cups whipping cream
2	cups half-and-half
¼	teaspoon celery seeds
¼	teaspoon ground white pepper
1	pound blue cheese, crumbled (we tested with Maytag)
2	large eggs
½	cup finely chopped fresh celery leaves
1	pound uncooked penne pasta
1	cup freshly grated Parmesan cheese

Melt 2 tablespoons butter in a large skillet over medium-high heat. Add peppers and celery; sauté 8 to 10 minutes or until crisp-tender. Sprinkle with salt. Set vegetables aside.

Melt ½ cup butter in a large saucepan over low heat. Add flour, whisking until smooth; cook 1 minute. Gradually add whipping cream and half-and-half; cook over medium heat, stirring constantly, until thickened. Whisk in celery seeds and white pepper. Remove from heat; add blue cheese, whisking until cheese melts.

Whisk eggs in a medium bowl until lightly beaten. Gradually whisk about one-fourth of hot white sauce into eggs, whisking constantly; add to remaining white sauce, stirring constantly. Whisk in celery leaves.

Cook pasta according to package directions; drain and return to pan. Stir in vegetables and white sauce. Pour into a lightly greased 13" x 9" baking dish. Sprinkle with Parmesan.

Bake, uncovered, at 400° for 30 minutes or until bubbly and lightly browned. Let stand 5 minutes before serving. Yield: 12 servings.

Cheese 'n' Chile Casserole

editor's favorite

Cheese 'n' Chile Casserole

Punch up the heat in this ultrarich brunch dish by using Monterey Jack cheese with peppers.

Prep: 18 min.   Cook: 45 min.   Other: 15 min.

9	large eggs
¾	teaspoon salt
3	(8-ounce) packages Monterey Jack cheese, cubed
2	(8-ounce) packages cream cheese, cubed
1	(12-ounce) container small-curd cottage cheese
1	tablespoon butter or margarine, cut into small pieces
¾	cup all-purpose flour
1½	teaspoons baking powder
1	(4.5-ounce) can chopped green chiles, drained
1	(2-ounce) jar diced pimiento, drained

Whisk together eggs and salt in a large bowl; add cheeses and butter. Whisk flour and baking powder into cheese mixture. Add green chiles and pimiento. Pour into a lightly greased 13" x 9" baking dish.

Bake, uncovered, at 350° for 45 minutes or until set. Let stand 10 to 15 minutes before serving. Yield: 16 servings.

Slow-Cooker Sensations

The slow cooker is ideal holiday equipment—it fills your home with inviting aromas, and it's hands-off cooking, allowing you to focus on family. Use it to make big batch candies, party dips and dessert, and classic soups and sides.

Triple Chocolate-Nut Clusters

Candy making has never been so easy! The slow cooker is the perfect tool to keep this candy mixture warm while you're spooning it out. (pictured at left)

Prep: 13 min.   Cook: 2 hrs.   Other: 2 hrs.

1   (16-ounce) jar dry-roasted peanuts
1   (9.75-ounce) can salted whole cashews
2   cups pecan pieces
18   (2-ounce) chocolate bark coating squares, cut in half
1   (12-ounce) package semisweet chocolate morsels
4   (1-ounce) bittersweet chocolate baking squares, broken into pieces
1   tablespoon shortening
1   teaspoon vanilla extract

Combine first 7 ingredients in a *5-quart slow cooker*; cover and cook on LOW 2 hours or until chocolate is melted. Stir chocolate and nuts; add vanilla, stirring well to coat.

Drop candy by heaping teaspoonfuls onto wax paper. Let stand at least 2 hours or until firm. Store in an airtight container. Yield: 6 dozen.

White Chocolate-Peppermint Jumbles

Salty pretzel nuggets are coated in white chocolate and combined with peppermints for an irresistible confection. (pictured at left)

Prep: 42 min.   Cook: 1 hr., 30 min.   Other: 1 hr.

2   (16-ounce) packages vanilla bark coating
1   (12-ounce) package white chocolate morsels
1   (6-ounce) package white chocolate baking squares
3   tablespoons shortening
1   (16-ounce) package pretzel nuggets (we tested with Snyder's of Hanover Sourdough Pretzel Nuggets)
1   (8-ounce) package animal-shaped crackers (3 cups)
1   cup coarsely crushed hard peppermint candies

Combine first 4 ingredients in a *6-quart slow cooker*. Cook, covered, on LOW 1 hour and 30 minutes or until vanilla bark and chocolate look very soft. Uncover and stir until smooth. Stir in pretzels, crackers, and crushed peppermint candies.

Drop candy by heaping tablespoonfuls onto wax paper. Let stand 1 hour or until firm. Yield: about 8 dozen.

Toffee Fondue

Save some fondue to spoon over ice cream.

Prep: 5 min.   Cook: 3 hrs.

¾   cup butter, cut into pieces
2   cups firmly packed light brown sugar
1¼   cups light corn syrup
3   tablespoons water
2   (14-ounce) cans sweetened condensed milk
¾   cup almond toffee bits
2   teaspoons vanilla extract
Pear slices
Pretzel rods
Shortbread sticks

Combine first 5 ingredients in a *4-quart slow cooker*. Cover and cook on LOW 3 hours, stirring occasionally, until fondue is smooth. Stir in toffee bits and vanilla. Serve with pear slices, pretzel rods, and shortbread sticks. Yield: 6 cups.

White Cheese Dip

Look for white American cheese in the deli department. We liked the extra spice contributed by 1 can of hot tomatoes—using 2 cans of regular tomatoes yields a much milder dip.

Prep: 11 min.   Cook: 2 hrs., 2 min.

1   small onion, finely chopped
3   garlic cloves, minced
1   (10-ounce) can hot diced tomatoes and green chiles
1   (10-ounce) can diced tomatoes and green chiles
1   (4.5-ounce) can chopped green chiles
½   teaspoon dried oregano
¼   teaspoon freshly ground pepper
2   pounds deli white American cheese, sliced (we tested with DiLusso)
1   cup milk

Place onion in a medium microwave-safe bowl; cover loosely with heavy-duty plastic wrap. Microwave on HIGH 2 minutes. Stir garlic and next 5 ingredients into onion.

Roughly tear cheese slices; place in a *4-quart slow cooker*. Pour milk over cheese; add onion mixture. Cover and cook on LOW 2 hours. Stir gently to blend ingredients. Yield: 8 cups.

Make Ahead: Spoon dip into serving-size freezer containers, and freeze up to 1 month. Thaw overnight in refrigerator. Reheat in microwave on MEDIUM (50%) power.

The Ultimate Party Crab Dip

It's ultimate because it's really rich and will serve a crowd for a holiday open house. Many newer slow cookers have a warm setting, which is perfect for keeping this dip hot throughout a party.

Prep: 32 min.   Cook: 2 hrs., 30 min.

2	tablespoons butter
6	green onions, chopped
2	garlic cloves, minced
1	cup heavy whipping cream
1	(14-ounce) can quartered artichoke hearts, drained and coarsely chopped
3	(8-ounce) packages cream cheese, softened
1	(8-ounce) can diced water chestnuts, drained
¾	cup chopped ham
½	cup shredded Parmesan cheese
2	tablespoons minced pickled jalapeño pepper slices or 1 fresh jalapeño, minced
¾	teaspoon salt
¼	teaspoon pepper
1	pound fresh lump crabmeat, drained
1	cup (4 ounces) shredded sharp Cheddar cheese

Melt butter in a large nonstick skillet over medium heat. Add green onions and garlic; sauté 4 minutes or until tender. Add cream and artichokes. Bring to a boil; reduce heat, and simmer 4 to 5 minutes or until reduced to 2 cups.

Beat cream cheese in a large bowl until smooth and creamy. Stir in water chestnuts and next 5 ingredients. Add artichoke cream sauce; stir until well combined. Gently fold in crabmeat.

Spoon dip into a lightly greased *3- or 4-quart slow cooker.* Sprinkle with Cheddar cheese. Cook, covered, on LOW 2½ hours or until thoroughly heated and cheese melts. Serve with toasted baguette slices or crackers. Yield: about 9 cups.

make ahead

Christmas Compote

Serve this orange-kissed, sweet-tart dessert topping warm or cold over ice cream or toasted pound cake.

Prep: 12 min.   Cook: 4 hrs.

6	large Golden Delicious apples, peeled, cored, and sliced
1	cup fresh or frozen cranberries
1	cup turbinado sugar
¼	cup orange marmalade
¼	cup cranberry-apple juice drink
¼	cup port
2	tablespoons Cointreau or other orange liqueur

Combine all ingredients in a *5-quart slow cooker.* Cover and cook on LOW 4 hours or until apples are tender. Cool. Serve warm or chilled. Yield: 4 cups.

editor's favorite

Sweet Potato Casserole

The slow cooker produces an undeniably good option for this favorite Southern holiday side dish.

Prep: 24 min.   Cook: 4 hrs.

2	(29-ounce) cans sweet potatoes in syrup, drained and mashed (about 4 cups)
⅓	cup butter or margarine, melted
⅔	cup firmly packed light or dark brown sugar
2	large eggs, lightly beaten
1	teaspoon vanilla extract
1	teaspoon ground cinnamon
⅓	cup whipping cream
1	cup coarsely chopped pecans
¾	cup firmly packed light or dark brown sugar
¼	cup all-purpose flour
2	tablespoons butter or margarine, melted

Combine first 6 ingredients in a large bowl; beat at medium speed with an electric mixer until smooth. Add cream; stir well. Pour into a lightly greased *3- or 4-quart oval-shaped slow cooker.*

Combine pecans and remaining 3 ingredients in a small bowl. Sprinkle over sweet potatoes. Cover and cook on HIGH 3 to 4 hours or until sugar melts on top of casserole. Yield: 8 cups.

Sweet Potato Casserole

Sprinkle chicken evenly with Caribbean rub; set aside.

Heat 1 teaspoon oil in a medium skillet over medium-high heat; add onion and garlic. Cook 3 minutes or until tender. Transfer mixture to a *5-quart oval slow cooker* using a slotted spoon. Heat remaining 3 teaspoons oil in skillet over medium-high heat; add chicken, and cook 6 to 8 minutes, or until browned, turning occasionally. Transfer chicken to slow cooker. Add 1 cup broth to skillet, scraping skillet to loosen browned bits. Pour over chicken. Add remaining broth, adobo sauce, and next 4 ingredients to slow cooker. Cover and cook on HIGH 1 hour. Decrease temperature to LOW, and cook 3 more hours.

Remove chicken from slow cooker, and cool 10 minutes. Remove chicken from bones, returning meat to slow cooker. Stir in lime juice. Serve soup over hot cooked rice; top with cilantro, radishes, and sour cream. Serve with lime wedges. Yield: 8 cups.

* We used adobo sauce from canned chipotle chiles in adobo sauce.

Caribbean-Style Chicken Soup with Lime and Cilantro

make ahead

Caribbean-Style Chicken Soup with Lime and Cilantro

A squeeze of lime, crisp radishes, and fresh cilantro add zing to this earthy soup.

Prep: 23 min.   Cook: 4 hrs.   Other: 10 min.

3   bone-in chicken breasts, skinned
3   bone-in chicken thighs, skinned
1   tablespoon salt-free Caribbean rub (we tested with Spice Hunter)
4   teaspoons vegetable oil
½   cup chopped onion
1   teaspoon minced garlic
1   (32-ounce) container chicken broth
1   tablespoon adobo sauce*
1   (15-ounce) can black beans, rinsed and drained
½   cup unsweetened coconut milk
1   teaspoon salt
½   teaspoon pepper
3   tablespoons fresh lime juice
Hot cooked rice
Fresh cilantro
Thinly sliced radishes
Sour cream
Lime wedges

Corn and Potato Chowder

Stop by the bakery for some rustic bread to accompany this hearty chowder.

Prep: 15 min.   Cook: 8 hrs.

1   pound baking potatoes, peeled and cut into ¼" cubes (about 2 cups)
1   (14.75-ounce) can cream-style corn
1   (14.5-ounce) can diced tomatoes
1   (14-ounce) can chicken broth
½   cup chopped onion
½   cup coarsely chopped celery
¾   teaspoon dried basil
½   teaspoon salt
¼   teaspoon pepper
1   bay leaf
1   cup whipping cream
¼   cup butter or margarine
4   bacon slices, cooked and crumbled

Stir together first 10 ingredients in a *5-quart slow cooker*. Cover and cook on LOW 8 hours or until potato is tender. Add whipping cream and butter, stirring until butter melts. Ladle into bowls; sprinkle each serving with bacon. Yield: 6 cups.

Fix it Faster: Cook bacon in the microwave or substitute packaged fully cooked bacon, prepared according to package directions.

Twice as Nice

Holiday recipes serve double duty in this chapter.
Each recipe is a delicious idea on its own, but look for another
suggested way to enjoy it in secondary recipes.

Brown Sugar Cake with Peanut Buttercream and Brittle Topping

(pictured at left)

Prep: 42 min.   Cook: 25 min.   Other: 10 min.

Old-Fashioned Peanut Brittle (recipe at right)
1½   cups butter, softened
2   cups firmly packed light brown sugar
6   large eggs
3   cups sifted cake flour
1   teaspoon baking powder
1   cup milk
2   teaspoons vanilla extract
Peanut Buttercream
½   cup semisweet chocolate morsels
2   tablespoons milk
1   tablespoon butter

Prepare Old-Fashioned Peanut Brittle.

Beat 1½ cups butter at medium speed with an electric mixer until creamy. Gradually add sugar, beating 7 minutes or until fluffy. Add eggs, 1 at a time, beating just until yellow disappears.

Combine flour and baking powder. Combine milk and vanilla. Gradually add alternately to butter mixture, beginning and ending with flour mixture. Beat at low speed just until blended after each addition. Spread batter into 2 greased and floured 9" cakepans.

Bake at 350° for 24 to 25 minutes or until a wooden pick inserted in center comes out clean. Cool in pans on wire racks 10 minutes. Remove from pans; cool on wire racks.

Break one-fourth of Old-Fashioned Peanut Brittle into 1½" to 2" pieces. Place an additional one-fourth of brittle in a large zip-top freezer bag; crush into coarse crumbs using a mallet or rolling pin. Reserve remaining brittle for another use.

Spread Peanut Buttercream between layers and on top and sides of cake. Press coarsely crushed brittle onto sides of cake.

Place chocolate morsels, milk, and 1 tablespoon butter in a small glass bowl. Microwave on HIGH 1 minute. Stir until smooth. Dip ends of peanut brittle pieces in chocolate ganache; place on wax paper to harden. Drizzle remaining ganache over cake. Arrange dipped brittle on top of cake. Yield: 1 (2-layer) cake.

Make-Ahead Note: Prepare the peanut brittle and cake layers a day ahead, or make the entire cake a day ahead. Either way, add chocolate-dipped brittle just before serving.

Peanut Buttercream

Prep: 6 min.

9   tablespoons butter, softened
¼   cup creamy peanut butter
½   cup milk
1½   teaspoons vanilla extract
5½   cups powdered sugar

Beat butter and peanut butter in a large bowl at medium speed with an electric mixer until blended. Combine milk and vanilla. Gradually add sugar and vanilla milk, 1 tablespoon at a time, beating until spreading consistency. Yield: 4 cups.

Old-Fashioned Peanut Brittle

We've perfected this classic candy with easy microwave directions. Follow the cook times closely based on the wattage of your microwave. Munch on half of the brittle, and use the rest in Brown Sugar Cake with Peanut Buttercream and Brittle Topping (recipe at left).

Prep: 7 min.   Cook: 9 min.

1   cup sugar
½   cup light corn syrup
⅛   teaspoon salt
1½   cups shelled raw peanuts
1   tablespoon butter
1   teaspoon vanilla extract
1   teaspoon baking soda

Microwave first 3 ingredients in a 2-quart glass bowl on HIGH 5 minutes, using an 1100-watt microwave oven. (Microwave 1 more minute if using a 700-watt microwave.) Stir in peanuts. Microwave 3 more minutes in an 1100-watt oven (add 1 more minute in 700-watt oven). Stir in butter and vanilla. Microwave 45 seconds in an 1100-watt oven (add 1 more minute in 700-watt oven) or until candy is the color of peanut butter. Stir in baking soda (mixture will bubble). Working quickly, spread hot candy in a thin layer onto a lightly greased baking sheet using two metal forks. Cool completely. Break candy into pieces. Yield: 1 pound.

Cranberry Liqueur

This makes an impressive gift any time of the year. Mix it with Champagne for an unexpected holiday treat or make our Holiday Martinis (recipe follows).

Prep: 10 min.   Cook: 5 min.   Other: 1 month

2¼   cups sugar
1   cup water
1   orange
1   pound fresh cranberries (4 cups)
4   cups vodka

Combine sugar and water in a medium saucepan; cook, stirring constantly, over medium heat 5 minutes or until sugar dissolves. Remove from heat, and cool completely.

Meanwhile, remove rind from orange with a vegetable peeler, being careful not to get the bitter white pith. Cut rind into strips, and set aside.

Process cranberries in a food processor 2 minutes or until very finely chopped. Combine sugar solution, orange rind, and cranberries in a 1-gallon jar; stir in vodka. Cover with lid, and store in a cool, dark place for 1 month.

Line a wire-mesh strainer with 2 layers of cheesecloth; strain liqueur through cheesecloth into a bowl. Discard solids. Carefully pour liqueur into clean bottles or jars. Yield: 5 cups.

Note: Cranberry Liqueur can be stored in a cool, dark place for up to a year.

editor's favorite • quick & easy
Holiday Martinis

Homemade Cranberry Liqueur replaces vodka in this pretty variation of a Cosmopolitan cocktail. (pictured on page 66)

Prep: 3 min.

⅓   cup cranberry juice cocktail
¼   cup Cranberry Liqueur (recipe above)
¼   cup Grand Marnier or Cointreau
1   tablespoon fresh lime juice
Garnish: twist of lime

Combine first 4 ingredients in a martini shaker; add ice cubes to fill container. Cover with lid, and shake 30 seconds or until thoroughly chilled. Remove lid, and strain into a martini glass. Serve immediately. Garnish, if desired. Yield: 1 serving.

editor's favorite
Sweet Potato-Butter Pecan Biscuits

These biscuits are great served alone, with ham, or as the base for the Winter Shortcakes (at right). We don't recommend substituting canned sweet potatoes in this recipe.

Prep: 17 min.   Cook: 1 hr., 21 min.

1   small sweet potato (about 8 ounces)
1   tablespoon butter or margarine
½   cup chopped pecans
2¼   cups all-purpose flour
1   tablespoon baking powder
½   teaspoon salt
½   cup cold butter, cut into pieces
½   cup sour cream
2   tablespoons light brown sugar
2   tablespoons maple syrup
2   tablespoons butter, melted

Scrub sweet potato; wrap in aluminum foil. Bake at 350° for 45 minutes to 1 hour. Cool completely. Scoop out pulp, and mash to equal ¾ cup. Set aside.

Melt 1 tablespoon butter in a small skillet over medium heat. Add pecans; cook, stirring constantly, 6 minutes or until toasted. Remove from heat; cool completely.

Combine flour, baking powder, and salt in a large bowl. Cut ½ cup butter into flour mixture with a pastry blender until crumbly; stir in pecans. Combine ¾ cup mashed sweet potato, sour cream, brown sugar, and maple syrup; add to flour mixture, stirring just until dry ingredients are moistened.

Turn dough out onto a heavily floured surface; knead 6 to 8 times, and pat into a 7" square (¾" thick). Cut dough into 9 squares; place squares 2" apart on a lightly greased baking sheet.

Bake at 425° for 15 minutes or until lightly browned. Brush with melted butter. Serve warm. Yield: 9 servings.

Fix it Faster: Pierce sweet potato skin with a knife, and microwave potato on HIGH 3 to 5 minutes; let stand 5 minutes after cooking. Bake or microwave sweet potato up to a day ahead, and mash. Chill overnight.

Winter Shortcakes

Winter Shortcakes

Prep: 14 min.   Cook: 21 min.

1	cup whipping cream
2	tablespoons powdered sugar
¼	teaspoon ground cinnamon
¼	cup butter
6	medium Granny Smith apples, peeled, cored, and sliced (about 7 cups)
1	cup sugar
½	cup chopped dates
1	teaspoon ground cinnamon
¼	teaspoon ground nutmeg
¼	teaspoon salt

Sweet Potato-Butter Pecan Biscuits (recipe at left)

Shortcake's not just meant for berries. This one sports a spiced apple filling piled onto a sweet potato biscuit.

Beat first 3 ingredients in a medium bowl at high speed with an electric mixer until soft peaks form. Cover and chill.

Melt butter in a large nonstick skillet over medium heat. Add apples and next 5 ingredients; cook over medium heat 20 minutes or until apples are tender, stirring often. Cool.

Split biscuits in half. Place biscuit bottoms on individual serving plates. Spoon ⅓ cup apple mixture evenly over each biscuit bottom. Place top half of each biscuit over filling. Spoon ⅓ cup apple mixture over biscuit top. Dollop with cinnamon whipped cream. Yield: 9 servings.

Gingerbread Biscotti

Bag these cookies for the ideal gift, but save enough to make the crust for Lemon Cheesecake (below).

Prep: 18 min.   Cook: 48 min.   Other: 15 min.

½   cup butter, softened
½   cup firmly packed light brown sugar
½   cup sugar
2   large eggs
¼   cup molasses
2½   cups all-purpose flour
1   teaspoon baking powder
1   teaspoon baking soda
1½   teaspoons ground ginger
1   teaspoon ground cinnamon
½   teaspoon ground nutmeg
¼   teaspoon ground cloves
¼   teaspoon salt
½   cup sliced almonds

Beat butter and sugars in a large bowl at medium speed with an electric mixer until light and fluffy. Add eggs, beating well; beat in molasses.

Combine flour and next 7 ingredients; add to butter mixture, beating at low speed until blended. Stir in almonds.

Divide dough in half; using floured hands, shape each portion into a 9" x 2" log on a lightly greased baking sheet.

Bake at 350° for 28 minutes or until firm. Cool on baking sheet 5 minutes. Remove to a wire rack to cool 10 minutes. Reduce oven temperature to 300°.

Cut each log diagonally into ¾"-thick slices with a serrated knife, using a gentle sawing motion. Place slices on ungreased baking sheets. Bake 8 to 10 minutes; turn cookies over, and bake 8 to 10 more minutes. Cool completely on wire racks. Yield: about 2 dozen.

Lemon Cheesecake

Prep: 27 min.   Cook: 1 hr.   Other: 9 hrs.

2   cups finely crushed Gingerbread Biscotti (recipe above)
¼   cup butter, melted
4   (8-ounce) packages cream cheese, softened
1½   cups sugar
1   (8-ounce) container sour cream
1   tablespoon cornstarch
4   large eggs
1   tablespoon grated lemon rind
⅓   cup fresh lemon juice
1   teaspoon vanilla extract

Gingerbread Biscotti

These crisp Italian cookies have a subtle ginger flavor; they're put to perfect use as a cheesecake crust.

Stir together crushed biscotti and butter in a bowl. Press cookie crumb mixture into bottom and 1" up sides of an ungreased 9" springform pan.

Bake at 325° for 10 minutes; let cool.

Meanwhile, beat cream cheese at medium speed with an electric mixer until creamy; gradually add sugar, beating well. Add sour cream and cornstarch, beating just until combined. Add eggs, 1 at a time, beating just until yellow disappears. Stir in lemon rind and remaining ingredients. (Do not overbeat.) Pour batter into baked crust.

Bake at 325° for 50 minutes or until set. Turn off oven. Immediately run a knife around edge of pan, releasing sides. Close oven door, and let cheesecake stand in oven 1 hour.

Remove from oven; cool completely in pan on a wire rack. Cover and chill 8 hours. Yield: 12 servings.

Homemade Caramel Sauce

Drizzle this golden sauce over Mile-High Turtle Ice Cream Pie (below), or serve as a topping for pound cake or ice cream.

Prep: 2 min. Cook: 12 min.

1¼   cups sugar
⅓   cup water
¾   cup whipping cream
⅓   cup butter, cut into pieces
½   teaspoon vanilla extract

Combine sugar and water in a large heavy saucepan; cook over medium-low heat, stirring often, until sugar dissolves. Increase heat to medium-high, and boil gently, without stirring, until syrup turns a deep amber color, occasionally brushing down sides of pan with a wet pastry brush and swirling pan (about 8 minutes). (Swirling the pan, instead of stirring, promotes more even cooking.) Gradually add cream (sauce will bubble vigorously). Add butter; stir gently until smooth. Remove from heat, and stir in vanilla. Yield: 1¾ cups.

Homemade Caramel Sauce

Mile-High Turtle Ice Cream Pie

Prep: 25 min.   Cook: 10 min.   Other: 6 hrs., 30 min.

2   cups chocolate cookie crumbs (about 40 cookies)
¼   cup butter or margarine, melted and cooled
2   pints dulce de leche ice cream, softened and divided (we tested with Häagen-Dazs)
1   cup Homemade Caramel Sauce (recipe above)
1½   cups chopped pecans, toasted and divided
1   pint chocolate ice cream, softened
1   (7-ounce) can sweetened whipped cream (we tested with Redi Whip)
¾   cup Homemade Caramel Sauce

Combine crumbs and melted butter in a small mixing bowl; stir well. Press crumbs in bottom of a 9" x 3" spring-form pan. Bake at 325° for 10 minutes. Cool completely.

Spoon 1 pint dulce de leche ice cream into cooled crust, and spread evenly; drizzle ⅓ cup Homemade Caramel Sauce over ice cream, and sprinkle with ¾ cup chopped pecans. Freeze 15 minutes or until ice cream is almost firm. Repeat procedure with chocolate ice cream, ⅓ cup Caramel Sauce, and remaining pecans; freeze until almost firm. Top with remaining dulce de leche ice cream and ⅓ cup Caramel Sauce. Cover and freeze 6 hours or up to 2 weeks in advance.

Mile-High Turtle Ice Cream Pie

Before serving, remove sides and bottom of pan; transfer pie to a serving platter. Top with sweetened whipped cream. Place ¾ cup Homemade Caramel Sauce in a microwave-safe bowl. Microwave at HIGH 1 minute or until warm. Drizzle 1 tablespoon sauce over each serving. Yield: 12 servings.

make ahead

Carnitas

Carnitas is a Mexican version of barbecue braised on the stovetop. Slowly simmered in broth or water, the meat becomes deliciously tender; then it's browned for a crisp exterior. Serve it plain or as tacos (see following recipe). Using a slow cooker delivers authentic results without watching the pot.

Prep: 16 min.   Cook: 6 hrs.

- 2   tablespoons tomato paste
- 2   tablespoons adobo sauce*
- 3   tablespoons chopped garlic
- 1   tablespoon chili powder
- 1   teaspoon salt
- 1   teaspoon pepper
- 3   pounds boneless Boston butt pork roast, cut into 2" pieces
- 1   cup beer or chicken broth

Combine first 6 ingredients in a *5-quart slow cooker*; stir in pieces of roast. Microwave beer in a 2-cup glass measuring cup on HIGH 2 minutes or until very hot. Pour beer over meat in slow cooker; do not stir. Cover and cook on HIGH for 6 hours or until very tender.

Shred meat using 2 forks. Serve hot or see notes below. Yield: 6 cups shredded meat.

* We used adobo sauce from canned chipotle chiles in adobo sauce.

Make-Ahead Note: Transfer meat mixture and juices to a 13" x 9" baking dish; cover and chill overnight. To reheat, crumble meat mixture into a large skillet, and cook over medium-high heat 15 minutes or until browned and hot.

Microwave Option: Traditionally, Carnitas are browned in their own drippings until they are crisped and browned. However, reheating the shredded pork in the microwave is an easy alternative. Microwave 6 cups meat mixture on HIGH 6 minutes, stirring once, or until thoroughly heated.

editor's favorite • quick & easy

Carnita Tacos

Consider a Carnita Taco supper during the holidays as an alternative to chili or soup. Set up the meal, buffet-style, and let everyone prepare their own taco with favorite toppings.

Prep: 10 min.

- 24   (6-inch) corn tortillas
- 6   cups Carnitas meat, warmed (recipe and instruction at left)

Toppings: queso fresco, chopped fresh cilantro, salsa verde, diced avocado, finely diced red onion, sour cream, lime wedges

Heat tortillas according to package directions. Place about ¼ cup Carnitas in center of each tortilla; top with desired toppings and a squeeze of fresh lime juice. Roll up tortillas; and serve immediately. Yield: 12 servings.

make ahead

Crabmeat Dip

This creamy dip doubles as an appetizer and a stuffing for boneless chicken breasts. It can easily be made a day ahead and baked just before guests arrive. Reserve ½ cup of the unbaked dip for Crabmeat-Stuffed Chicken Breasts.

Prep: 22 min.   Cook: 30 min.

- 1   (8-ounce) package cream cheese, softened
- 1   (5.2-ounce) package buttery garlic-and-herb spreadable cheese (we tested with Boursin)
- ½   cup mayonnaise
- ¼   cup finely chopped red bell pepper
- ¼   cup chopped green onions
- ¾   cup freshly grated Parmesan cheese
- 1   teaspoon coarse-grained Dijon mustard
- ½   teaspoon Worcestershire sauce
- 1   teaspoon hot sauce
- 2   tablespoons fresh lemon juice
- 1   garlic clove, minced
- 2   tablespoons capers
- ¼   teaspoon freshly ground black pepper
- 1   pound fresh lump crabmeat, drained

Combine first 13 ingredients, stirring well. Gently fold in crabmeat. Spoon dip into a lightly greased 8" square baking dish. Bake at 350° for 30 minutes or until bubbly. Serve with crackers or Melba toast rounds. Yield: 4½ cups.

Crabmeat-Stuffed Chicken Breasts

Prep: 12 min. Cook: 33 min.

4   skinned and boned chicken breasts
¼   teaspoon salt
½   teaspoon freshly ground pepper
½   cup uncooked Crabmeat Dip (recipe at left)
¾   cup loosely packed fresh spinach leaves
4   slices prosciutto, cut into 7" x 4" strips
2   teaspoons olive oil

Place each chicken breast between 2 sheets of heavy-duty plastic wrap; pound to ¼" thickness using a meat mallet or rolling pin. Sprinkle chicken with salt and pepper.

Spread 2 tablespoons Crabmeat Dip over each chicken breast. Divide spinach evenly over dip; roll up chicken, jelly-roll fashion. Wrap each roll with 1 slice prosciutto; secure with a wooden pick.

Heat oil in an ovenproof skillet over medium-high heat. Add chicken, and cook 3 to 4 minutes on each side or until prosciutto is lightly browned and crispy. Place skillet in oven, and bake at 350° for 25 minutes or until chicken is done. Remove wooden picks before serving. Yield: 4 servings.

Note: Make Crabmeat Dip no more than 1 day ahead of preparing Crabmeat-Stuffed Chicken Breasts.

Walnut Mashed Potatoes

Toasted nuts give fresh appeal to these spuds. Save 4 cups of the unbaked potatoes for the Shepherd's Pie recipe that follows.

Prep: 25 min. Cook: 35 min.

6   pounds baking potatoes, peeled and cut into 1" cubes (about 8 large potatoes)
¾   cup butter or margarine, cut into pieces
1½   cups half-and-half
2   teaspoons salt
½   teaspoon pepper
4   green onions, chopped
1½   tablespoons olive oil
1¼   cups chopped walnuts, toasted

Cook potatoes in boiling water to cover 30 minutes or until tender; drain well. Return potatoes to pan. Add butter, and mash with a potato masher. Add half-and-half, salt, and pepper. Mash again to desired consistency.

Sauté green onions in hot oil in a medium skillet over medium-high heat 5 minutes or until crisp-tender. Add onions and walnuts to mashed potato, stirring until blended. Yield: 14½ cups.

Note: Chop walnuts by hand for this recipe instead of using a processor because a processor often creates "dust" that can discolor the potatoes.

Shepherd's Pie

This down-home casserole has a fast prep and the comfort-food appeal of a one-dish dinner.

Prep: 5 min. Cook: 44 min.

1   pound ground beef
¾   cup chopped onion
1½   teaspoons olive oil
2   tablespoons all-purpose flour
1⅓   cups water
2   teaspoons beef bouillon granules
1   teaspoon Worcestershire sauce
¼   teaspoon salt
¼   teaspoon pepper
2   cups frozen mixed vegetables, thawed and patted dry
4   cups unbaked Walnut Mashed Potatoes (recipe at left)
¼   cup freshly grated Parmesan cheese
Paprika

Cook ground beef in a large skillet, stirring until it crumbles and is no longer pink; drain well, and set aside. Wipe skillet clean.

Sauté onion in hot oil in skillet over medium-high heat until tender. Add flour, stirring well; stir in water. Cook, stirring constantly, over medium-low heat, until thickened. Add bouillon and next 3 ingredients, stirring well. Add beef and thawed vegetables; stir well.

Spoon beef mixture into a lightly greased 2-quart casserole dish. Spread Walnut Mashed Potatoes over beef mixture; sprinkle with Parmesan cheese. Lightly sprinkle with paprika.

Bake, uncovered, at 350° for 30 minutes or until hot and bubbly. Yield: 4 servings.

Seasonal Pantry Favorites

Cranberries, vanilla, and coconut—3 holiday
pantry staples—are highlighted in these recipes.

Chocolate-Almond-Coconut Macaroons

These cookies are even scrumptious unadorned. (pictured at left)

Prep: 18 min.   Cook: 22 min.

1   (14-ounce) package sweetened flaked coconut
¾   cup sweetened condensed milk
½   (7-ounce) package almond paste, grated (we tested with Odense)
2   tablespoons all-purpose flour
½   teaspoon vanilla extract
½   teaspoon almond extract
½   teaspoon grated orange rind
¼   teaspoon salt
¼   cup semisweet chocolate mini-morsels
1   egg white
½   cup semisweet chocolate morsels (optional)
1   tablespoon shortening (optional)
¼   cup sliced almonds, toasted (optional)

Combine coconut and sweetened condensed milk in a large bowl. Add almond paste and next 5 ingredients. Stir in mini-morsels.

Beat egg white at high speed with an electric mixer until stiff peaks form; fold into coconut mixture.

Drop by heaping tablespoonfuls onto parchment paper-lined baking sheets.

Bake at 325° for 20 to 21 minutes or until edges are golden and tops are lightly browned. Cool completely on baking sheets.

If desired, microwave chocolate morsels and shortening in a 1-cup glass measuring cup on HIGH 1 minute or until melted, stirring once.

Pour melted chocolate into a small zip-top freezer bag. Snip a small hole in 1 corner of bag; drizzle chocolate over macaroons, and sprinkle with toasted almonds, if desired. Let stand until chocolate is firm. Yield: 2 dozen.

Coconut-Cranberry Trifle

Convenience products simplify this holiday trifle. The hard part is waiting four hours for it to chill.

Prep: 23 min.   Cook: 5 min.   Other: 4 hrs., 45 min.

1   (16-ounce) can whole-berry cranberry sauce
1   (12-ounce) jar red currant jelly (we tested with Crosse & Blackwell)
2   tablespoons grated orange rind (rind of 2 oranges)
1   tablespoon cornstarch
3   (3.4-ounce) packages coconut cream or vanilla instant pudding mix
4   cups milk
1   (16-ounce) frozen pound cake, thawed, cut into 1" cubes, and divided
6   tablespoons Grand Marnier, divided
1½ cups sweetened flaked coconut, toasted and divided
2   cups frozen whipped topping, thawed

Combine first 4 ingredients in a medium saucepan. Bring to a boil over medium heat; cook 1 minute or until thickened and bubbly. Chill 45 minutes or until completely cooled, stirring occasionally.

Combine pudding mix and milk in a large bowl; whisk 2 minutes or until thickened.

Place one-third of pound cake cubes in a 3-quart trifle bowl; drizzle with 2 tablespoons liqueur. Top with one-third of cranberry-orange sauce and one-third of pudding. Sprinkle with ½ cup coconut.

Repeat layers twice using remaining cake cubes, orange liqueur, cranberry-orange sauce, pudding, and coconut, reserving last ½ cup coconut for garnish.

Spread whipped topping over trifle. Sprinkle with reserved coconut. Cover and chill at least 4 hours. Yield: 12 servings.

gift idea

Coconut-Chocolate Pastries

These candy-filled pillows make a nice gift from the kitchen along with a bag of gourmet coffee.

Prep: 35 min.   Cook: 12 min. per batch   Other: 5 min.

½   (8-ounce) package cream cheese, softened
½   cup powdered sugar
1   teaspoon vanilla extract
1   cup sweetened flaked coconut
1   (17.3-ounce) package frozen puff pastry sheets, thawed
5   (1.55-ounce) milk chocolate candy bars, broken into
    sections
1   large egg
1   tablespoon water
Powdered sugar

Beat cream cheese at medium speed with an electric mixer in a medium-sized bowl until creamy. Add ½ cup powdered sugar and vanilla; beat until smooth. Stir in coconut.

Roll 1 sheet puff pastry into a 12" x 12" rectangle. (Pastry will be thin.) Cut into 9 (4") squares. Stack 2 chocolate sections, just off center, on each square; top chocolate with 1 heaping teaspoon coconut mixture.

Whisk together egg and water in a small bowl. Lightly brush edges of squares with egg mixture; fold into triangles. Seal edges with a fork. Place pastries on parchment paper-lined baking sheets.

Repeat procedure with remaining sheet of pastry, chocolate (reserve extra chocolate sections for another use), and coconut mixture. Brush remaining egg wash over top of pastries.

Bake at 400° for 12 minutes or until golden. Cool on baking sheets 5 minutes; transfer to wire racks to cool completely. Sift powdered sugar over pastries. Yield: 1½ dozen.

Toasted Coconut-Chocolate Chunk Pecan Pie

editor's favorite • make ahead

Toasted Coconut-Chocolate Chunk Pecan Pie

A long, slow bake time yields deep-dish chocolate paradise.

Prep: 7 min.   Cook: 1 hr., 15 min.

1   (15-ounce) package refrigerated piecrusts
⅓   cup butter or margarine, melted
1   cup sugar
1   cup light corn syrup
4   large eggs, lightly beaten
1   teaspoon vanilla extract
¼   teaspoon salt
1½   cups pecan halves
1   cup sweetened flaked coconut, toasted
¾   cup semisweet chocolate chunks or morsels

Unroll 1 piecrust, and place on a lightly floured surface; lightly brush top of crust with water. Unroll remaining crust, and place over bottom crust; gently roll into a 10" circle. Fit into a 9" deep-dish pieplate; fold edges under, and crimp.

Stir together butter and next 5 ingredients in a large bowl; stir well. Stir in pecans and remaining ingredients. Pour filling into piecrust.

Bake at 325° for 1 hour and 15 minutes or until set, shielding crust after 45 minutes with aluminum foil, if necessary. Cool completely on a wire rack. Yield: 8 to 10 servings.

Coconut-Chocolate Pastries

editor's favorite • gift idea • make ahead

White Chocolate-Dipped Oatmeal-Cranberry Cookies

Prep: 46 min.   Cook: 11 min. per batch

1 cup butter or margarine, softened
1 cup firmly packed light brown sugar
½ cup granulated sugar
1 large egg
1 tablespoon vanilla extract
2 cups all-purpose flour
1 teaspoon baking soda
½ teaspoon baking powder
½ teaspoon salt
2 cups sweetened dried cranberries (we tested with Craisins)
1½ cups pecan pieces, toasted
1¼ cups uncooked quick-cooking oats
3 (4-ounce) white chocolate baking bars, coarsely chopped (we tested with Ghirardelli)
3 tablespoons shortening

Beat butter at medium speed with an electric mixer until creamy; gradually add sugars, beating well. Add egg and vanilla, beating until blended.

Combine flour and next 3 ingredients; gradually add to butter mixture, beating until blended. Stir in cranberries, pecans, and oats.

Drop dough by heaping tablespoonfuls 2" apart onto lightly greased baking sheets.

Bake at 375° for 9 to 11 minutes or until lightly browned. Cool on baking sheets 2 minutes. Transfer to wire racks to cool completely.

Microwave white chocolate and shortening in a medium-size microwave-safe bowl on HIGH 1 minute or until chocolate melts, stirring once. Dip half of each cookie into melted chocolate, letting excess drip back into bowl. Place dipped cookies on wax paper; let stand until firm. Yield: about 4 dozen.

Dipping these chunky cookies into white chocolate adds a special holiday touch, but they're great plain, too.

White Chocolate-Dipped Oatmeal-Cranberry Cookies

make ahead

Cranberry-Couscous Salad

Pair this cinnamon-scented side with grilled chicken or lamb.

Prep: 10 min.   Cook: 4 min.   Other: 5 min.

1½   cups chicken broth
½   cup dried cranberries
1   teaspoon ground cinnamon
¼   teaspoon ground cumin
1   cup uncooked couscous
⅓   cup vegetable or canola oil
2   tablespoons rice vinegar
½   cup sliced almonds, toasted
⅓   cup chopped green onions
2   tablespoons chopped fresh mint or parsley
Red leaf lettuce leaves

   Combine first 4 ingredients in a medium saucepan; bring to a boil. Remove from heat, and stir in couscous. Cover and let stand 5 minutes. Fluff with a fork; let cool, uncovered.

   Whisk oil and vinegar; pour vinaigrette over couscous. Add almonds, green onions, and mint; toss well. Serve at room temperature or chilled over red leaf lettuce. Yield: 6 servings.

make ahead

Holiday Granola Bars

Prep: 20 min.   Cook: 40 min.

¼   cup butter or margarine, softened
½   cup firmly packed light brown sugar
1   large egg, lightly beaten
½   cup honey
½   cup vanilla yogurt
1   teaspoon vanilla extract
1   cup all-purpose flour
1   teaspoon ground cinnamon
½   teaspoon baking powder
¼   teaspoon salt
1½   cups uncooked quick-cooking oats
1¼   cups crisp rice cereal
1   cup dried cranberries
½   cup sliced almonds
½   cup chopped pecans
½   cup sunflower seed kernels
2   tablespoons sesame seeds

   Beat butter at medium speed with an electric mixer until creamy. Gradually add sugar, beating until light and fluffy. Add egg, beating well. Stir in honey, yogurt, and vanilla.

   Combine flour and next 3 ingredients in a large bowl. Stir in oats and remaining ingredients; add to butter mixture, stirring well. Press mixture into a foil-lined 13" x 9" pan coated with cooking spray.

   Bake at 350° for 35 to 40 minutes or until lightly browned. Cut into bars while warm. Cool completely in pan on a wire rack. Store in an airtight container up to 5 days. Yield: 2 dozen.

Note: Always taste nuts and sunflower seeds before using in a recipe. If not stored properly, they become rancid quickly.

editor's favorite

Brown Sugar-Pecan Cupcakes

Satisfy your sweet tooth with the delicate crunch of brown sugar and pecans that top these little cakes.

Prep: 32 min.   Cook: 22 min.

¾   cup chopped pecans
¼   cup butter or margarine, softened
¼   cup shortening
1   cup granulated sugar, divided
3   large eggs, separated
2   teaspoons vanilla bean paste
1   cup all-purpose flour
½   teaspoon baking soda
½   cup buttermilk
¼   cup firmly packed light brown sugar
Browned Butter Frosting

   Bake pecans in a shallow pan at 350°, stirring occasionally, 8 minutes or until toasted. Cool completely. Process ¼ cup pecans in a food processor until finely chopped. Set aside.

   Beat butter and shortening at medium speed with an electric mixer until fluffy; gradually add ¾ cup granulated sugar, beating well. Add egg yolks, 1 at a time, beating until blended after each addition. Stir in vanilla bean paste.

   Combine flour and baking soda; add to butter mixture alternately with buttermilk, beginning and ending with flour. Beat at low speed until blended after each addition.

   Beat egg whites at medium speed until soft peaks form; add remaining ¼ cup granulated sugar, 1 tablespoon at a time, beating until stiff peaks form. Fold one-third of egg whites into batter; fold in remaining egg whites and ½ cup toasted pecans. Spoon batter into paper-lined muffin cups, filling two-thirds full.

   Bake at 350° for 22 minutes or until a wooden pick inserted in center comes out clean. Cool in pans 5 minutes on a wire rack. Remove from pans, and cool completely.

Combine reserved ¼ cup finely chopped pecans and brown sugar in a small bowl. Spread a generous 2 tablespoons Browned Butter Frosting onto each cupcake. Sprinkle tops of cupcakes with pecan-sugar mixture. Yield: 18 cupcakes.

Browned Butter Frosting

There's no substitute for butter in this recipe. Only browned butter achieves the nutty flavor that makes this unique frosting so good.

Prep: 8 min.   Cook: 4 min.   Other: 20 min.

¼   cup butter
1   (8-ounce) package cream cheese, softened
1   (16-ounce) package powdered sugar
1½   teaspoons vanilla bean paste

Cook butter in a small heavy saucepan over medium heat, stirring constantly, 3 to 4 minutes or until browned. Transfer to a large mixing bowl, and chill 20 minutes.

Add cream cheese to browned butter; beat at medium speed until smooth. Gradually add powdered sugar, beating until light and fluffy. Stir in vanilla bean paste. Yield: 2¾ cups.

the essence of vanilla

We recommend using vanilla bean paste in these cupcakes. It has a speckled, syrupy consistency. Find it at Williams-Sonoma or other cook stores. If you want to substitute, the conversions are: 1 tablespoon vanilla bean paste= 1 tablespoon vanilla extract=1 whole vanilla bean.

Brown Sugar-Pecan Cupcakes

Easy Ideas for
Creative Decorating

Let the dozens of delightful decorations on these pages
inspire you to have the most magical holiday home ever.

A Mantel for

Style the mantel for the harvest changes, and it's

Autumn Color

Begin this double-duty design by gathering items that work for both autumn and Christmas (see photo at right). Try containers, candleholders, and a scarf or length of fabric to add softness. Then decide on a focal point, such as a wreath, that can be switched easily to change the seasonal look of the mantel (see pages 94 and 95).

Tuck richly colored leaves and berries into the arrangement along the mantel, allowing naturals to softly drape over the mantel's edge.

Fill containers with branches of persimmon and bittersweet to add height to the arrangement and to balance the design.

For a cheerful glow, punctuate the mantel with candles. Be sure to keep greenery and dried plants away from candle flames and never leave candles burning unattended.

Two Seasons

season; then make a few quick
ready for Christmas.

Christmas Greenery

After celebrating Thanksgiving, replace the focal point
with a Christmas wreath. We used a magnolia wreath
with twigs and berries (see pages 96 and 97). As an alternative to two different wreaths, for autumn, stick
fall-colored leaves and dried seedpods into an unadorned
grapevine wreath; for Christmas, replace the leaves and
dried materials with evergreen clippings and berries.

Replace the autumn leaves, and fill in
around the candles with small bouquets of natural materials, such as
magnolia leaves, berries, eucalyptus,
and mossy twigs.

Use tall stems with red berries and moss-
covered branches in a glass container to
reflect the wreath's embellishments and to
add a dramatic extra punch of color and
texture.

For Christmas, replace the harvest
candles with holiday candles, varying
heights for interest. Form collars of
pepperberries, seeded eucalyptus, or
moss around the base of the candles
for a fancy finish.

Harvest Mantel

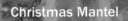

Retro Chic

Blend new and vintage accents for a casual yet elegant look that's all about comfort and charm.

◀ Gather the Goods

Pull together a fresh, traditional style from a hodgepodge of common household accessories, vintage pieces, and flea-market finds. Use new items, such as the stockings and ornaments shown here, to kick-start the theme; then fill in with mood-setting elements, such as the candleholders, old window frame, and chair. The abundant garland, with its delicate plumosa fern fronds and lemon leaves, suits the cozy mood.

▼ No Bow Required

Set your creativity free when trimming the holiday wreath. Here, dried hydrangea blooms fill the center of the wreath, creating an interesting color contrast that makes additional embellishments unnecessary.

Soft-hued wrappings match the room's vintage decorations. Feel free to wrap holiday presents in colors other than red and green. Using papers and ribbons from your year-round supply is also less expensive. Incorporate unusual elements: try rickrack in place of ribbon, or create a cummerbund with paper to give gift wrap even more personality.

One favorite item—such as the **Victorian-style stocking shown here**—can influence your decorative holiday choices, from ornaments to gift wrappings.

Custom Blend

Use similar colors and materials to coordinate mantel and table decorations. Dried hydrangea is featured in both the centerpiece and mantel wreath. Soft red napkins, moss green place mats, and neutral table coverings reflect the stockings' hues and the easygoing elegance of the entire design.

Easy Does It

A cake stand stacked atop a taller stand creates a centerpiece foundation with
height and presence without obstructing guests' views across the table. To suit your
theme, fill in with such materials as fresh and dried hydrangea blooms (as shown
here), pinecones, greenery, ornaments, wrapped boxes, or votive candles.

Mixing and matching glasses, plates, and flatware that share a common mood is key to this casual, chic look. Here, dressy plates are white, stemmed glasses are clear, and etched glasses turned upside down act as votive holders at place settings. A clip-on bird ornament adds a fanciful note.

Easy, Earthy Style

Deck your halls with colors that complement your home's decor. As these rooms reveal, a blue-and-brown scheme is right at home at the holidays.

◀ Strong Carry Through

On the table, blue pottery and candles, bronze candleholders and chargers, and blue-and-brown ornaments also used on the living room mantel reinforce the decorative link between the two places of interest.

▼ Clearly a Good Idea

Glass vases and jars are invaluable assets when it comes to decorating—anytime of year. For Christmas, fill a clear container with ornaments or fruits. On this mantel, ornament-filled cylinders add height and balance to the arrangement.

Choose one of your favorite objects to suggest your holiday palette. The earthy colors and woodsy feel of the painting above are repeated in the blue-and-brown mantel decorations. The smooth surfaces of the ornaments and bronze finials provide congenial counterpoints to the rustic textures of the evergreen twigs, pinecones, and birch-bark reindeer.

Continue your decorating scheme
right down to the party favors. Here, a feathery
ornament awaiting a lucky dinner guest is a
handsome addition to the tablescape.

◄Center of Attention

For an inexpensive alternative to flowers, accent a centerpiece with feathers—they're
showy, fun, and reusable. To make a similar arrangement, place moistened florist
foam in a bowl. Arrange the feathers first, and then fill in with evergreen cuttings,
artichokes, and ornaments. The florist foam helps keep the greenery looking fresh
for several days.

Garden-Style Greetings

Use potted plants and fragrant greenery for a fresh and easy approach to holiday trimmings.

▲ Super Simple

Layer kumquats and reindeer moss to make a cheery candle decoration in a glass urn. Also try this idea using cranberries or unshelled nuts.

Good Scents ▶

Any room you use a lot deserves holiday embellishments. This sunroom, a favorite gathering place, calls for easy-going and fresh materials. Evergreen wreaths in the windows and pots of paperwhites and amaryllis around the room add fragrant accents.

◄ Pot Holders

For a quick centerpiece, think potted plants. Here, maidenhair ferns and bromeliads in decorative containers surround a folk-art tree. Dine on informal plates in earthy colors to complement the casual garden motif.

Grow Your Own

Forcing paperwhite bulbs to bloom is easy.

You will need: glass container • pebbles • paperwhite bulbs

1 Fill the bottom of a glass container with pebbles. Add water up to the top of the pebbles. Place the paperwhite bulbs on top.

2 Keep the container consistently filled with water so that the bottoms of the bulbs are just touching the water. Keep the bulbs in a cool, dark area for the first week to promote root growth; then move them to a warmer spot with bright light. The bulbs will begin growing immediately and will bloom in four to six weeks.

3 Sow a succession of paperwhites every week in the fall for a continuous display of blooms all winter.

In keeping with the garden theme,
treat each guest to a tiny tool party
favor tied to a napkin.

◄Branch Out

When decorating for the holidays, include favorite pieces of art in the mix. This folk-art tree, which usually resides in the home's foyer, is a perfectly charming accent for the Christmas breakfast table.

Magnolia Place Mats

Create one-of-a-kind table accents from magnolia leaves.

You will need: magnolia leaves • liquid glycerin (optional) • canvas or cardboard cut into oval shapes • low-temp glue gun and glue sticks

1 If desired, preserve the magnolia leaves' appearance by submerging them in a solution of liquid glycerin (available at crafts stores; follow manufacturer's directions for preserving leaves). Or place the magnolia leaves underneath a heavy stack of books to press them flat (without the glycerin step, the leaves may begin to curl after a few days).

2 Arrange the leaves on top of the canvas or cardboard backing, and glue them in place.

Display wrapped gifts to build
holiday anticipation and excitement.

Right at Home ▶

There's no need to replace everyday accessories when dressing a room for
the holidays. In this sunny corner, birdhouses on a sideboard fit the festive
mood with the addition of red berries and an evergreen garland and wreath.

Fresh Greens

Bright yellow-green accents add sparkle to a traditional setting.

▲ Twinkle, Twinkle

Jazz up an evergreen garland by placing a glittery garland on top of the greenery. For even more sparkle, tuck in frosted ornaments among the garlands and also dangle them along the edges of the mantel to catch the twinkle of lights in the room.

Pretty in Red and Green ▶

Here, the table and mantel are perfect partners with such repeating elements as the red and green flowers, ornaments, and tableware. Chartreuse updates this traditional color combination on the place mats and ball trim, salad plates, and flowers.

◀ Special Addition

Step up the glamour on the mantel with vases of fresh flowers. To give the room's decorations a harmonious appearance, use the same types of flowers in all arrangements. In the room pictured here, we used amaryllis, orchids, and variegated holly.

▲ Easy Accent

Tie a Christmas stocking to the back of each dining chair as a decorative way to offer party favors.

Fancy Place Mats
Create a lively table setting by encircling place mats with beaded garlands.

Wine Caddy Centerpiece

Keep your options open when choosing a centerpiece container. Here, a wooden wine caddy serves up style.

You will need: container • florist foam • small wreath • flowers and berries • greenery clippings

1 Fill the container with moistened florist foam; then place a small wreath on top of the container. (We used a glittery wreath, but a small evergreen wreath will work, too.)

2 Nestle the flowers and berries in the center of the wreath, and press the stems into the florist foam.

3 Fill in around the wreath with the greenery clippings. The wreath helps hold the arrangement in place and forms a pretty collar around the flowers.

Winsome Windows

Here are five fabulous ideas for framing festive views.

▲Suitable Stand-in

If you don't have deep windowsills to hold plants, consider using a freestanding plant container in front of a window. For this arrangement, mingle potted conifers with artificial bottlebrush trees. Fill in the gaps between the trees with oversize pinecones and ornaments. Finish with a big bow tied with wire-edge ribbon.

Snow Scene ▶

Layer on the white to create a frosty setting. Place a flocked garland on the windowsill, and then add such white accents as pillar candles and vases filled with paperwhites and hyacinth blooms. Position silver ornaments among the garland to pick up the twinkle of the candles. For the final wintry flourish, use double-sided tape to stick snowflakes on the windowpanes.

◀ Cherubs and Chartreuse

An unusually deep kitchen windowsill allows plenty of space for a fanciful holiday windowscape. The unexpected mix of dressy bronze pieces with diminutive chartreuse urns is made even more playful with the addition of wheatgrass and pansies. This same setup would also make an attractive sideboard decoration—just be sure not to place the grass directly on wooden or painted surfaces.

A Wreath in Minutes

An evergreen wreath is a classic Christmas decoration. Instead of the usual round shape, try this rectangular version that uses a picture frame as a base.

You will need: picture frame • green florist wire • greenery clippings or garland

1 Select an inexpensive picture frame to use as the wreath form. (Check out crafts and discount stores, flea markets, and tag sales. The condition of the frame doesn't matter because it will be covered by greenery.)

2 Use green florist wire to attach the greenery or garland to the frame. Completely cover the frame with the greenery. If you plan to hang the wreath in a window, be sure to cover the back of the frame, too.

3 Store the frame to reuse next year.

Introduce unexpected elements in
your window decorations for picture-perfect views.

Cool Beans

Red and green jelly beans bring fun to this simple window design. Using a two-color theme helps the various pieces work together for a well-planned look.

Showcase your favorite
ornaments by hanging them
from ribbons to create a colorful,
whimsical window treatment.
Thread an end of each ribbon
through an ornament loop; then
glue the cut end to the back of
the ribbon. Use thumbtacks to
attach the ribbons at the top
of the window.

Inspiration Point

Plan your holiday decorating scheme around something you love.
Here, this tablecloth is a stunning start to a grand design.

◀ A Good Beginning

Try a floor-length tablecloth to transform a table for the
season. After selecting the tablecloth, choose table and
mantel accents that complement its mood and colors.
The feather-trimmed tablecloth shown here inspired
glamorous gold and feather accessories.

▲ Fine Details

Carry the motif from the table to the mantel to enhance
the theme. Here, the gold bottlebrush trees are joined by
feather trees and glittery conifers that become the build-
ing blocks for the fireplace decoration. Red ribbons,
berries, and fruits fill in with bursts of color.

◄ More Is Better

Layer accents for maximum impact. Deep red candles, roses, napkins, and pears are a rich contrast to the moss green tablecloth. Glistening gold trees and ornaments pump up the glitz. Vertically placed place mats add color and texture while protecting the tablecloth from spills.

▲A Little Something Extra

Crisscross the table with bands of wide ribbon, letting the ends trail over the sides. Pin, glue, or tack ornaments to the trailing ribbons for an unexpected adornment.

Passion for Plates

Some of the most versatile holiday decorating items are in your kitchen cabinet. Be inspired to showcase your plates in an entirely new setting.

Neutral Noel

Pair white dinnerware with snappy accents to set a Christmassy scene. Nestle rich red flowers and fruits against the neutral backdrop for a strong contrast, and finish with touches of chartreuse for an extra pop of color.

Create a refined woodsy ambience with plates in earthy tones complemented by wispy pine branches, rich mocha ornaments, and pottery angels. Tie a sheer ribbon to one of the branches for an airy contrast.

▲ Lighten Up

Fill an assortment of wineglasses, juice glasses, and votive holders with candles to add a merry twinkle to an array of plates; note how varying the heights of the candles creates a more pleasing setup. Tuck greenery and berry stems among the plates and candles for a finished look.

Quick Transfer ▼

It takes only a few elements to change an arrangement from ho-hum to holiday. Add holiday charm to a display of classic brown-and-white transferware by propping gingerbread snowflake cookies in plate stands and centering a single snowflake ornament on a serving platter. (Silver dragées on the cookies are for decoration only.)

Star Power

Give this seasonal icon a starring role for whimsical charm.

Whether on the tree or underneath it, stars are the bright spots of the season.

◀ Catch a Star

A starfish in a glass urn filled with rock salt and sprinkles of dragées is a surprisingly elegant design. For a different look, consider accenting with a snowflake or crystal ornament instead of the starfish. One urn encircled with a crimson feather wreath works nicely on a round table; for a rectangular table, line up several urns along the length of the table. This decorating idea also works well on a mantel.

Frame a Star

Dangle star ornaments in an empty frame to fill a wall with cheer.

You will need: ribbon • star ornaments • thumbtacks • picture frame (without glass)

1 Cut the ribbon into varying lengths, and thread them through the hanging loops on the ornaments.

2 Use the thumbtacks to attach the ribbons to the top back edge of the frame.

To complete the scene, balance additional stars in glass candle-holders and sprinkle them along the mantel. Light candles to make the whole arrangement shine.

Season-Spanning Shine

These star-shaped tea light lanterns make a glowing centerpiece that lasts all season. Blocks of colored florist foam cut to fit this open-weave container make it easy to position the stars and berries. Bright ornaments fill in around the blocks of foam.

A Big Star

This oversize piece is truly the star of the show. Use one king-size decoration, such as this star, instead of several small items for a quick design that has loads of impact.

A Merry Welcome

Spruce up the guest room with Christmassy
accents for a cheery retreat.

◄ Comfort and Joy

Consider these suggestions to make holiday visitors feel refreshed and at ease. Place a holiday-inspired accent pillow and red throw on the bed—both will be appreciated by a tired traveler. Replace framed artwork with evergreen wreaths. Switch everyday lampshades with shades in seasonal colors. String bead garlands along the tops of windows for a festive window treatment. Stand a cheerfully decorated tree in a corner.

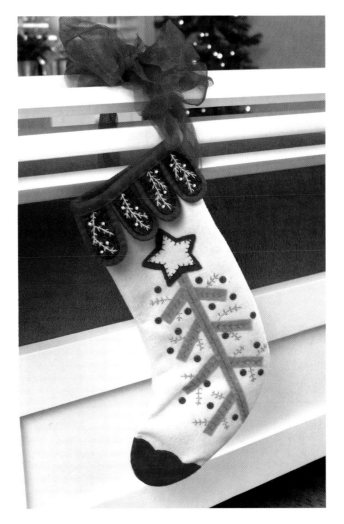

Goodies for Your Guest

A stocking filled with little luxuries makes a guest feel welcome. Consider these items for stocking stuffers that pamper and please.

- An aromatherapy candle with evergreen or cinnamon scent
- A brightly colored mug and hot cocoa mix
- Lollipops or chocolates for a sweet indulgence
- A gourmet tea infuser for a cozy cup of tea

Do-It-Yourself
Holiday Style

Express your distinctive flair with decorations
you make yourself. The photos and directions
on these pages show you how.

Decorating Classics in 3 Easy Steps

Whether looking for an exquisite bow to trim a gift or the best way to embellish a plain wreath, you'll discover step-by-step photos that reveal how to decorate like a pro.

Decorate a Wreath

Transform a wreath from blah to breathtaking with the simple addition of wired-on bows and bouquets.

You will need: wire-edge ribbon • evergreen wreath • thumbtack • dried flowers • berries • wooden florist picks with wires • florist tape and wire • ornaments

1 Use a length of ribbon to hang the wreath, tacking the ribbon in place at the top of the door.

2 To make each bouquet, attach dried flowers and berries to a wooden florist pick with wires. (We used dried hydrangea blooms and pepperberries.) Wrap the stems with florist tape to secure each bouquet. Wire several small bouquets to the wreath.

3 To make each bow for the wreath, form 2 loops from a length of ribbon. Cinch the center of the bow with a wooden florist pick with wires. Stick several bows in the wreath, filling in among the flowers. Wire ornaments to the wreath for pops of color.

Tie a Package Bow

A well-tied bow is the secret to a beautiful package.

You will need: wire-edge ribbon • wrapped package

1 Center the middle of a length of ribbon on top of the package. Wrap the ribbon down 2 sides of the box, cross it underneath the box, and bring it back up the other 2 sides. Tie the ribbon in a knot on top of the package, leaving several inches for the tails.

2 Starting about 4 inches from the end of a length of ribbon, make a loop. Pinching the ribbon between your thumb and index finger, make a loop on the opposite side; repeat to make 2 loops on each side.

3 Center the bow on top of the package, and secure it in place by tying the ribbon tails around it. Fluff the loops to shape the bow.

Make a Big Bow

This is the classic bow for decorating. Use it on garlands, on wreaths, and even as a tree topper.

You will need: 5 to 6 yards wire-edge ribbon • florist wire

1 Starting about 8 to 10 inches from the end of a length of ribbon, make a loop. Pinching the ribbon between your thumb and index finger, make a loop on the opposite side.

2 Continue making loops in this back-and-forth manner until you are happy with the fullness of the bow.

3 Tie a length of ribbon around the center of the bow, making the knot on the back of the bow. Let the ribbon tails fall from the bow, and fluff the loops to shape the bow. Use florist wire to attach the bow where desired.

Create a Floral Centerpiece

Styling a professional-looking centerpiece is as easy as 1–2–3.

You will need: florist foam • container • flowers • pillar candle •
berries • greenery sprigs • wire-edge ribbon

1 Place moistened florist foam in the container. Stick the stems of the flowers into the foam, forming a collar around the top of the container.

2 Center a pillar candle on the florist foam. Stick the stems of the berries around the candle. (We used pepperberries.) Fill in any gaps with sprigs of greenery.

3 Tie a bow around the candle, securing small blooms in the knot.

Quick-as-a-Wink Centerpieces

These tabletop accents can be arranged in minutes, thanks to
the handy materials lists and easy directions.

◄ Stacked Packages

You will need: 2 cake stands (one larger than the other) • small, wrapped boxes • berries • greenery sprigs

1 Place the smaller cake stand atop the larger stand.

2 Arrange the wrapped boxes on the cake stands; place a tallish box in the center of the small cake stand to give the centerpiece a pleasing shape.

3 Tuck the berries and wispy sprigs of greenery, such as cedar or cypress, among the boxes.

Tiers of Fruit ►

You will need: assorted fruits • tiered compote • holly berries or herb sprigs

1 Arrange the fruits on each tier of the compote. (If you are using grapes, allow them to drape over the edges.)

2 Add a few stems of the holly berries to the arrangement for decoration only (the berries are non-edible); or tuck sprigs of fragrant herbs, such as rosemary or lavender, among the pieces of fruit.

◄ Ornament Collection

You will need: container • tissue paper (optional) • assorted ornaments • hypericum berries • greenery clippings

1 For a large container, fill the bottom of the container with crumpled tissue paper. Arrange a variety of ornaments in the container, using different shapes and styles to add interest.

2 Fill in around the edges of the arrangement and among the ornaments with the berries and greenery. (A box similar in size to the one pictured is best suited for a sideboard decoration; for a dining table, choose a bowl or basket that's low enough for guests to see across.)

Flowers and Ornaments

You will need: vases in various heights • assorted flowers, berries, and greenery clippings (we used amaryllis, seeded eucalyptus, tulips, anemones, ranunculus, fir clippings, and holly berries) • ornaments • (the gift boxes are ornaments)

1 Arrange the vases, and fill with the flowers, berries, and greenery clippings. Group similar colors for maximum impact.

2 Scatter the ornaments around the vases to tie the arrangement together.

More Ideas for Centerpieces

- Fill silver serving pieces with red carnations. Using one color makes an impressive presentation. ▸
- For a twinkling design, place tea lights on a tiered compote.
- To save money on flowers, use large blooms. For example, place a few calla lilies in a glass vase; add a couple of votive candles on each side of the vase for an elegant yet inexpensive table decoration.
- Instead of decorating with a large centerpiece, mark each place setting with a small vase filled with a few flowers, a sprig of greenery, and a snip of berries. Be sure to cut the stems short so that the materials hug the tops of the vases.

Party-Ready Centerpiece

You will need: punch bowl, cups, and tray • holiday garland • small evergreen wreaths •
tall cake stands with domes • small cakes or cookies • ribbons • flowers and berries • wrapped boxes

1 Set the punch bowl and cups on a large tray at the center of the table. Weave a holiday garland around the cups (see pages 156 and 157).

2 Place the small wreaths on each side of the punch bowl. Set a cake stand in the center of each wreath. Place decorated cakes or stacks of cookies on the cake stands.

3 Tie together small bouquets of flowers and berries with the ribbon. Lay the bouquets on the wreaths for colorful accents. Fill in along the back of the arrangement with the wrapped boxes.

Pillows with Pizzazz

Give plain pillows extreme makeovers that are specially suited to the season.

◄ Stocking Pillow

You will need: fabric for stocking •
hot-glue gun and glue sticks • plain pillow • yarn trim for
stocking • trim for cuff • fake fur for cuff • tassels

1 Draw a stocking shape on the reverse side of the
fabric, and cut it out. Hot-glue the stocking to
the pillow.

2 Hot-glue the yarn trim along the edges of the stocking. Hot-glue the cuff trim to the top of the stocking.
Hot-glue the cuff to the pillow, covering the top edge of
the trim.

3 Stitch the tassels to the stocking toe and to each
pillow corner.

Wreath Pillow ►

You will need: hot-glue gun and glue sticks •
looped chenille trim • plain pillow •
small pompoms • ribbon

1 Hot-glue 2 rows of the chenille trim (to double the
width) in a circle on the pillow.

2 Hot-glue the pompoms randomly on the wreath.

3 Tie the ribbon in a bow. Hot-glue the bow to the top
of the wreath.

Snowflake Pillow ►

You will need: hot-glue gun and glue sticks •
narrow white trim • plain pillow • buttons •
white pompom trim

1 Hot-glue the narrow trim to the pillow, using the
photo at right as inspiration.

2 Hot-glue a large button to the center of the pillow
where the trim intersects. Hot-glue a small button to
the end of each point of the snowflake.

3 Hot-glue the pompom trim around the edges of
the pillow.

Spotlight on Shades

**Turn on a holiday look when you switch plain
lampshades with these dressed-up versions.**

Hand-Lettered Shade

You will need: pencil • ivory lampshade • fine-tip permanent black fabric pen • hot-glue gun and glue sticks • beaded trim

1 With a pencil, lightly mark a rule for the line spacing at the overlap area on the shade. Use the fabric pen to write seasonal sentiments on the shade. If you prefer not to write the words freehand, use adhesive letters, quotes, or stencils (found in the scrapbooking section of crafts and discount stores) for a similar effect.

2 Hot-glue the trim to the top and bottom of the shade.

Drummer-Boy Shade ▶

You will need: pencil • red drum-shaped lampshade • ribbons • small paintbrush • thick craft and fabric glue

1 Use a pencil to lightly mark the placement of the ribbons on the lampshade. Cut the ribbons to desired lengths.

2 Use the paintbrush to spread glue on the back of the ribbons. Glue the zigzag design first; then glue the ribbons to the top and bottom of the shade.

Holly and Berries Shade ▶

You will need: heavy paper, such as thick wrapping paper, handmade paper, or wallpaper • thick craft and fabric glue • ivory drum-shaped lampshade • black sequins

1 Using the photo at right as inspiration, cut out the designs from the heavy paper.

2 Glue the cutouts to the lampshade. Glue the black sequins in place to accent the holly-berry designs.

Old Fashioned
Peanut Brittle

Share the Spirit of the Season

These pages will inspire you to treat everyone on your list to cleverly packaged gifts from the kitchen, handmade party invitations, and stylishly coordinated wrappings.

You're invited to a
Cookie Swap!

Saturday
December 10th
2-4 p.m.

Caroline's house
54 Peachtree Lane

RSVP 613-4296

Wrapped in Style

When you give gifts from your kitchen, you'll want
them to look as good as they taste. Here are some simple ideas.

Instant Spiced Tea Mix, page 37
Citrus Curd, page 36

Thoughtfulness takes on a special meaning during the holidays. In the hustle and bustle of such busy times, taking a moment to deliver homemade treats brightens the season and spreads the joy. Here are a few tips and gift-giving ideas.

• Purchase a wide selection of jars, buckets, and decorative tins at grocery and variety stores. Also check out tag sales for bargain-priced containers.
• Decorate jar lids with festive fabric scraps, colored or textured tissue papers, or napkins. Cut with decorative-edge scissors to fit, if desired.
• Shop crafts stores for small kitchen utensils and decorations to tie on packages.
• Generate recipe cards on the computer using colored paper stock and kitchen-themed designs.
• Wash a potato chip, drink mix, or mixed nuts container. Glue fabric around the container, or spray-paint the container. Glue ribbon or fabric trim around the bottom of the container. Spray-paint the plastic lid, if desired. Fill the container with cookies, and cover with the plastic lid.

Triple Chocolate-Nut Clusters, White Chocolate-Peppermint Jumbles, page 73

Gingerbread Biscotti, page 80

Homemade Caramel Sauce, page 81

Goodies for Giving

Select any of the following for scrumptious food gifts this holiday season.

• Triple Chocolate-Nut Clusters (page 73)
• White Chocolate-Peppermint Jumbles (page 73)
• Old-Fashioned Peanut Brittle (page 77)
• Homemade Caramel Sauce (page 81)
• Chocolate-Almond-Coconut Macaroons (page 85)
• Coconut-Chocolate Pastries (page 86)
• White Chocolate-Dipped Oatmeal-Cranberry Cookies (page 87)

JOIN US FOR A CUP OF WASSAIL
AFTER AN EVENING OF CAROLING

SUNDAY, THE SIXTEENTH OF DECEMBER

THE ELLIOTS

REGRETS ONLY   455-5497

...NDLE AND YOUR SINGING VOICE
...N US FOR AN EVENING OF CAROLING
DECEMBER 21ST
7 PM
THE GRANTS

Irresistible Invitations

**Sending preparty favors with invitations makes
the offer so fetching that it's impossible to refuse!**

Using the invitations shown here and on page 163 as inspiration, visit the scrapbooking sections at local crafts and discount stores to gather colored papers, pens, die-cut shapes, decorative-edge scissors, and ribbons. (Also check out Internet sites, such as michaels.com, for supplies.)

Cute Combos

• Pair holiday cookie cutters with invitations to a cookie swap.
• Hand-deliver holiday mugs to announce a wassail party.
• Send candles along with invitations to light the way for a night of caroling.
• Adorn plastic champagne flutes with an invitation to a New Year's Eve soiree.

Easy, Artsy Gift Tags

Use die cuts and simple geometric shapes to create perfectly coordinated gift tags for your packages.

Gift Tag How-tos

You will need: spray adhesive • decorative papers • cardstock • decorative-edge scissors (optional) • assorted trims

1 Use spray adhesive to adhere decorative papers to the fronts of cardstock.

2 Cut out such shapes as stars, trees, holly leaves, bells, and stockings from cardstock, using decorative-edge scissors if desired.

3 Mount the shapes to tags made from folded or trimmed cardstock. Add trims to finish the tags.

Where to Find It

Source information is current at the time of publication; however, we cannot guarantee availability of items. If an item is not listed, its source is unknown.

12 Menus of Christmas

page 10—covered bowl: Vagabond Vintage Furniture; Atlanta, GA; (404) 351-6484

page 13—plates: Lamb's Ears Ltd.; Birmingham, AL; (205) 969-3138

page 17—cake pedestal: Pot Luck Studios; (800) 559-7341; www.potluckstudios.com

pages 18–19—ball ornament place card holder: Christine's; Mountain Brook, AL; (205) 871-8297; **snowflake place card holders:** Henhouse Antiques; (205) 918-0508; www.shophenhouseantiques.com

page 25—ramekins: Crate & Barrel; (800) 967-6696; www.crateandbarrel.com

page 26—plate and linen: Lamb's Ears Ltd.; Birmingham, AL; (205) 969-3138

page 31—place card holders: Target; www.target.com

pages 38–39—napkins: Secret Garden Embroidery; Plano, TX; (972) 618-7284; www.secretgardenemb.com; **bowls and place mats:** Lamb's Ears Ltd.; Birmingham, AL; (205) 969-3138

page 46—bowls, plates, and chargers: Pottery Barn; (888) 779-5176; www.potterybarn.com

page 53—plates and linens: Lamb's Ears Ltd.; Birmingham, AL; (205) 969-3138

page 57—ornaments: Christmas & Co.; Birmingham, AL; (205) 823-6640; www.christmasandco.com; **plates and chargers:** Bromberg & Co.; (800) 633-4616; www.brombergs.com; **napkin:** Table Matters; Mountain Brook, AL; (205) 879-0125; www.table-matters.com

page 58—tray: Godinger; (800) 544-2209; www.godinger.com; **table runner:** Christine's; Mountain Brook, AL; (205) 871-8297

pages 60–61—cake pedestal: Godinger; (800) 544-2209; www.godinger.com; **dessert plates:** Bromberg & Co.; (800) 633-4616; www.brombergs.com

page 64—napkins: Smith Variety; Birmingham, AL; (205) 871-0841; **tray:** Table Matters; Mountain Brook, AL; (205) 879-0125; www.table-matters.com; **plate:** Lamb's Ears Ltd.; Birmingham, AL; (205) 969-3138

Season's Best Recipes

pages 66–67—martini glass: Z Gallerie; (800) 358-8288; www.zgallerie.com; **casserole dish and caddy:** Gracious Goods; Overland Park, KS; (866) 238-6448; www.graciousgoods.net

page 71—casserole caddy: Lamb's Ears Ltd.; Birmingham, AL; (205) 969-3138

page 74—polka-dot tray and bowls:
Lamb's Ears Ltd.; Birmingham, AL;
(205) 969-3138

Easy Ideas for Creative Decorating

page 90—pillow: Linda Wright;
Birmingham, AL;
throw: Pottery Barn; (888) 779-5176;
www.potterybarn.com;
stocking: Christmas & Co.;
Birmingham, AL; (205) 823-6640;
www.christmasandco.com

**pages 92–97—candles and
candleholders:** Pottery Barn;
(888) 779-5176; www.potterybarn.com;
urns: *Southern Living At HOME®;*
www.southernlivingathome.com
for ordering information;
table runner: Lamb's Ears Ltd.;
Birmingham, AL; (205) 969-3138

**pages 98–99—stockings and
ornaments:** Anthropologie;
Birmingham, AL; (205) 298-9929;

window frame: Tricia's Treasures;
Homewood, AL; (205) 871-9779;
candleholders: At Home;
Homewood, AL; (205) 879-3510;
tall candleholders: Tricia's Treasures;
Homewood, AL; (205) 871-9779

page 100—wrapping paper: Frontier;
Athens, GA; (706) 369-8079

**page 101—plates and green table
linens:** Anthropologie; Birmingham,
AL; (205) 298-9929;
table runner: Harmony Landing;
Homewood, AL; (205) 871-0585

**pages 104–109—place mats, chargers,
plates, and napkins:** Table Matters;
Mountain Brook, AL; (205) 879-0125;
www.table-matters.com;
flatware: Pottery Barn; (888) 779-5176;
www.potterybarn.com;
glassware: Flora; Homewood, AL;
(205) 871-4004;
candleholders and pitcher: *Southern
Living At HOME®;*
www.southernlivingathome.com
for ordering information;
centerpiece container: Lamb's Ears Ltd.;
Birmingham, AL; (205) 969-3138;
chairs: Mulberry Heights Antiques;
Birmingham, AL; (205) 870-1300;
pillows: Target; www.target.com;

feather ornaments and feathers:
Harmony Landing; Homewood,
AL; (205) 871-0585;
pitcher on mantel: Lamb's Ears Ltd.;
Birmingham, AL; (205) 969-3138;
finials: *Southern Living At HOME®;*
www.southernlivingathome.com
for ordering information;
reindeer: Harmony Landing;
Homewood, AL; (205) 871-0585;
stocking holders: Target;
www.target.com;
glass containers: *Southern Living
At HOME®;*
www.southernlivingathome.com
for ordering information;
lichen ball: Harmony Landing;
Homewood, AL; (205) 871-0585

pages 110–117—glass urn:
Southern Living At HOME®;
www.southernlivingathome.com
for ordering information;
centerpiece tree: Connie Methvin;
Bremen, AL;
plates, glassware, and napkins:
World Market; (877) 967-5362;
www.worldmarket.com;
place favors: Smith & Hawken;
(800) 940-1170;
www.smithandhawken.com;
green roof birdhouse: Harmony Landing;

Homewood, AL; (205) 871-0585;
other birdhouses: *Southern Living
At HOME®;*
www.southernlivingathome.com
for ordering information;
monogram on chair cover: Topstitchin';
Birmingham, AL; (205) 943-8440

**pages 118–123—bead garland,
centerpiece wine caddy, and wreath
in centerpiece:** Lamb's Ears Ltd.;
Birmingham, AL; (205) 969-3138;
place mats, napkins, and glassware:
Table Matters; Mountain Brook, AL;
(205) 879-0125; www.table-matters.com;
plates: Macy's; www.macys.com;
balls around place mats: Lamb's Ears
Ltd.; Birmingham, AL; (205) 969-3138;
stocking: Lamb's Ears Ltd.;
Birmingham, AL; (205) 969-3138;
mesh flower container on mantel:
Christmas & Co.; Birmingham,
AL; (205) 823-6640;
www.christmasandco.com

pages 124–125—garland and tree:
Rosegate Designs, Inc.; (205) 321-1345;
ribbon: Christmas & Co.; Birmingham,
AL; (205) 823-6640;
www.christmasandco.com;
large green ornaments: Dorothy
McDaniel's Flower Market; Homewood,
AL; (205) 871-0092

**pages 126–127—candleholders and
urn:** Mulberry Heights Antiques;
Birmingham, AL; (205) 870-1300;
wreath: Davis Wholesale
Florist; (205) 595-2179;
candles: Christine's; Mountain
Brook, AL; (205) 871-8297

pages 128–129—candleholder:
Mulberry Heights Antiques;
Birmingham, AL; (205) 870-1300;
ornaments: The Christmas Tree;
Pelham, AL; (205) 988-8090; Seasons
of Cannon Falls™ brand holiday and
seasonal home accents are available
in gift, specialty, and department
stores across the country. To locate a
retailer near you, please visit
www.seasonsofcannonfalls.com, and
click on "Where to Shop;" or call
(800) 377-3335

pages 130–133—tablecloth:
The Christmas Tree; Pelham,
AL; (205) 988-8090;
plates, red chargers, cups, and saucers:
Bromberg & Co.; (800) 633-4616;
www.brombergs.com;
napkin rings: Macy's; www.macys.com;
**glassware, place mats, and twig
trees:** Table Matters; Mountain
Brook, AL; (205) 879-0125;
www.table-matters.com;
feather trees: Silk in Design;
Birmingham, AL; (205) 252-4711;
beaded trees: Lamb's Ears Ltd.;
Birmingham, AL; (205) 969-3138;
napkins: Pottery Barn; (888) 779-5176;
www.potterybarn.com

pages 134–135—all pitchers and serving ware: Mulberry Heights Antiques; Birmingham, AL; (205) 870-1300

pages 136–137—transferware and snowflake ornament: Mulberry Heights Antiques; Birmingham, AL; (205) 870-1300;
cookies: Angels Cake & Confections; Mountain Brook, AL; (205) 871-3536; AngelsConfection@bellsouth.net
plates: Table Matters; Mountain Brook, AL; (205) 879-0125; www.table-matters.com;
angels: A'Mano; Birmingham, AL; (205) 871-9093;
snowman plates and green wineglass: Vietri; (866) 327-1279; www.vietri.com

pages 138–139—urn: *Southern Living At HOME*®; www.southernlivingathome.com for ordering information;
tree skirt: Garnet Hill; (800) 870-3513; www.garnethill.com;
ornaments: Christmas & Co.; Birmingham, AL; (205) 823-6640; www.christmasandco.com

pages 140–141—candles: Christmas & Co.; Birmingham, AL; (205) 823-6640; www.christmasandco.com

pages 142–143—lanterns and ornaments, star, wreath stand holding star, star ornaments, and star bowls: Pier 1 Imports; (800) 245-4595; www.pier1.com

Do-It-Yourself Holiday Style

pages 146–147—vases: Vietri; (866) 327-1279; www.vietri.com;
package ornament: The Christmas Tree; Pelham, AL; (205) 988-8090

pages 148–149—evergreen wreath: Sugar Mountain Nursery & Landscape; (800) 892-7440; www.sugarmtnnursery.com;
dried materials for wreath: Harmony Landing; Homewood, AL; (205) 871-0585;

copper chafing dish container: Tricia's Treasures; Homewood, AL; (205) 871-9779

page 150—evergreen garland: Sugar Mountain Nursery & Landscape; (800) 892-7440; www.sugarmtnnursery.com

pages 152–153—green tumblers: A'Mano; Birmingham, AL; (205) 871-9093;
Santa ornaments: Christmas & Co.; Birmingham, AL; (205) 823-6640; www.christmasandco.com;

tiered compote: Godinger; (800) 544-2209; www.godinger.com

page 154—chairs: Mulberry Heights Antiques; Birmingham, AL; (205) 870-1300

pages 155–157—cakes: Angels Cake & Confections; Mountain Brook, AL; (205) 871-3536; AngelsConfection@bellsouth.net;
red berry wreath: Lamb's Ears Ltd.; Birmingham, AL; (205) 969-3138;
cake stands: Mulberry Heights Antiques; Birmingham, AL; (205) 870-1300;
star plates: Williams-Sonoma; (877) 812-6235; www.williams-sonoma.com;
punch bowl and cups: Godinger; (800) 544-2209; www.godinger.com;
bead garland: Christmas & Co.; Birmingham, AL; (205) 823-6640; www.christmasandco.com

Share the Spirit of the Season

page 164—vintage jars: Kmart; (866) 562-7848; www.kmart.com;
napkin linen: Lamb's Ears Ltd.; Birmingham, AL; (205) 969-3138;
ribbon: Smith Variety; Birmingham, AL; (205) 871-0841

Recipe Index

Almond Torte with Cranberry Jam, 28
Appetizers
  Beef and Blue Sandwiches with
    Caramelized Onions, 63
  Black-eyed Pea Cakes with Cranberry-
    Red Pepper Salsa, 45
  Chicken Won Ton Cups, Asian, 64
  Crostini, Smoked Trout and Pecan, 12
  Dips
    Cheese Dip, White, 73
    Crab Dip, The Ultimate Party, 74
    Crabmeat Dip, 82
  Mushroom Puffs, Easy, 63
  Salsa, Cranberry-Red Pepper, 45
  Sandwiches, Turkey Finger, 35
  Scallop Ceviche, 63
  Spread, Blue Cheese, 64

Banana Nut and Dulce de Leche Coffee
  Cake, 52
Beans, Balsamic, 16
Beans with Ham and Cream, Lima, 32
Beans with Roasted Shallots, Green, 21
Beef
  Pie, Shepherd's, 83
  Prime Rib with Horseradish Cream, 24
  Sandwiches with Caramelized Onions,
    Beef and Blue, 63
  Tenderloin with Madeira, Bacon-
    Wrapped Beef, 14
Beverages
  Alcoholic
    Berry Fizz, 52
    Cranberry Liqueur, 78
    Margaritas, Pomegranate, 62
    Martinis, Holiday, 78
  Tea Mix, Instant Spiced, 37
Biscuits, Rosemary, 49
Biscuits, Sweet Potato-Butter Pecan, 78
Breads. *See also* Biscuits, Cornbread, Muffins.
  Ginger-Honey Bread, 36
  Scones, Buttery, 36
Broccoli with Balsamic Butter, 42
Brussels Sprouts with Marmalade
  Glaze, 54

Cabbage Sauté, Chestnut and Red, 31
Cabbage with Garlic Cream, Grilled Red, 16

Cakes
  Brown Sugar Cake with Peanut
    Buttercream and Brittle Topping, 77
  Cheesecake, Lemon, 80
  Chocolate Chunk Cherry Cake, Dark, 16
  Chocolate Layer Cake, Dark, 60
  Coffee Cake, Banana Nut and Dulce de
    Leche, 52
  Cupcakes, Brown Sugar-Pecan, 88
  Petits Fours, Gingerbread, 65
  Pumpkin-Pecan Layer Cake, 47
  Shortcakes, Winter, 79
  Torte with Cranberry Jam, Almond, 28
Candies
  Clusters, Triple Chocolate-Nut, 73
  Jumbles, White Chocolate-
    Peppermint, 73
  Peanut Brittle, Old-Fashioned, 77
  Truffles, Pumpkin Pie, 65
Carrot Puree with Browned Butter and
  Ginger, 24
Carrots, Ginger-Rum, 21
Casseroles
  Cheese 'n' Chile Casserole, 71
  Gumbo Casserole with Creamed Garlic
    Shrimp, 69
  Ham-and-Hash Brown Breakfast
    Casserole, 51
  Mac and Cheese, Chic, 71
  Potatoes, Roasted Garlic and Herb, 21
  Spanakopita, Deep-Dish, 69
  Strata, Pizza, 70
  Sweet Potato Casserole, 74
Cauliflower Bisque, 18
Cherry Cake, Dark Chocolate Chunk, 16
Cherry Sauce, Dried, 33
Chicken
  Garlic, Chicken with 40 Cloves of, 41
  Mac and Cheese, Chic, 71
  Soup with Lime and Cilantro,
    Caribbean-Style Chicken, 75
  Stuffed Chicken Breasts, Crabmeat-, 83
  Walnut Chicken with Dijon Cream
    Sauce, 54
  Won Ton Cups, Asian Chicken, 64
Chocolate
  Bread Pudding, Chocolate, 25
  Cake, Dark Chocolate Chunk Cherry, 16

  Cake, Dark Chocolate Layer, 60
  Fondue, Bittersweet Chocolate, 65
  Frosting, White Chocolate, 60
  Jumbles, White Chocolate-
    Peppermint, 73
  Panini, Chocolate, 43
  Pastries, Coconut-Chocolate, 86
  Pots de Crème, Chocolate-Espresso, 42
  Rice Pudding with Dried Cherry Sauce,
    White Chocolate, 32
Chowder, Corn and Potato, 75
Coconut
  Macaroons, Chocolate-Almond-
    Coconut, 85
  Pastries, Coconut-Chocolate, 86
  Pie, Toasted Coconut-Chocolate
    Chunk Pecan, 86
  Trifle, Coconut-Cranberry, 85
Cookies
  Bars, Holiday Granola, 88
  Biscotti, Gingerbread, 80
  Cigarillos, Molasses, 55
  Macaroons, Chocolate-Almond-
    Coconut, 85
  Oatmeal-Cranberry Cookies, White
    Chocolate-Dipped, 87
Corn and Potato Chowder, 75
Cornbread, Apple-Cheddar, 32
Cranberries
  Jam, Cranberry, 28
  Liqueur, Cranberry, 78
  Martinis, Holiday, 78
  Salad, Cranberry-Couscous, 88
  Salsa, Cranberry-Red Pepper, 45
Croutons, Rosemary, 31

Desserts. *See also* specific types.
  Compote, Christmas, 74
  Curd, Citrus, 36
  Fondue, Bittersweet Chocolate, 65
  Fondue, Toffee, 73
  Panini, Chocolate, 43
  Pots de Crème, Chocolate-
    Espresso, 42
  Sauce, Dried Cherry, 33
  Sauce, Homemade Caramel, 81
  Spread, Pink Princess, 37
  Trifle, Coconut-Cranberry, 85

Frostings and Toppings
  Browned Butter Frosting, 89
  Citrus Curd, 36
  Ginger-Cream Cheese Frosting, 47
  Horseradish Cream, 24
  Peanut Buttercream, 77
  White Chocolate Frosting, 60
Fruit with Ginger Syrup, Tropical, 52

Grits, Gruyère, 47

Ham-and-Hash Brown Breakfast
  Casserole, 51
Ham with Mustard-Peach Glaze,
  Baked, 59

Jam, Cranberry, 28

Kale with Roasted Garlic, Wilted, 28

Lamb with Pineapple-Pecan Salsa,
  Sage-Crusted Leg of, 27
Lasagna, Roasted Vegetable, 70

Muffins, Cheddar and Green
  Onion, 54
Mushroom Puffs, Easy, 63
Mushroom Salad, Roasted, 27

Onions
  Caramelized Onion and Mushroom
    Bisque, 44
  Caramelized Onions, 64
  Green Onion Muffins, Cheddar
    and, 54
Orzo, Lemon, 28
Oyster Stew with Rosemary Croutons, 30
Oysters with Red Pepper Romesco,
  Cornmeal-Crusted, 26

Pea Cakes with Cranberry-Red Pepper
  Salsa, Black-eyed, 45
Pecans, Maple Mashed Squash with
  Candied, 32
Peppers
  Chile Casserole, Cheese 'n', 71
  Red Pepper Romesco, 27
  Red Pepper Salsa, Cranberry-, 45
Pies, Puffs, and Pastries
  Coconut-Chocolate Chunk Pecan Pie,
    Toasted, 86
  Ice Cream Pie, Mile-High Turtle, 81
  Shepherd's Pie, 83

Spanakopita, Deep-Dish, 69
Puffs, Easy Mushroom, 63
Tarts
  Caramel Chess Tart, 22
  Shells, Tartlet, 56
  Shrimp and Benne Seed Tartlets, 56
  Spinach and Gruyère Tarts, 49
  Tassies, Caramel Chess, 22
Pineapple-Pecan Salsa, 27
Pizza Strata, 70
Pomegranate Margaritas, 62
Pork
  Carnitas, 82
  Carnita Tacos, 82
  Roast with Chestnut and Red Cabbage
    Sauté, Brined Pork, 31
  Sausage Patties, Fresh Pork, 49
Potatoes. See also Sweet Potatoes.
  Hash Brown Breakfast Casserole,
    Ham-and-, 51
  Herb Potatoes, Roasted Garlic
    and, 21
  Mashed Potatoes, Walnut, 83
  Smashed Potatoes, Herb-Parmesan, 42
  Soup, Potato-Leek, 23
Puddings
  Bread Pudding, Chocolate, 25
  Butterscotch Pudding with Bourbon-
    Brown Sugar Meringue, 55
  Rice Pudding with Dried Cherry Sauce,
    White Chocolate, 32
  Yorkshire Puddings, Blue Cheese, 24
Pumpkin-Pecan Layer Cake, 47
Pumpkin Pie Truffles, 65

Rice Pudding with Dried Cherry Sauce,
  White Chocolate, 32

Salads and Salad Dressings
  Baby Romaine and Blood Orange
    Salad, 12
  Bean Salad with Olives, Warm, 40
  Butter Lettuces with Chutney
    Vinaigrette, 53
  Cranberry-Couscous Salad, 88
  Green Salad with Cranberry-
    Champagne Vinaigrette, 20
  Mushroom Salad, Roasted, 27
  Romaine Salad with Walnut-Champagne
    Vinaigrette, Hearts of, 48
  Slaw, Fennel, Apple, and Celery, 59
  Sweet Potato Salad with Bacon
    Vinaigrette, 59

Salsa, Cranberry-Red Pepper, 45
Salsa, Pineapple-Pecan, 27
Sandwiches
  Beef and Blue Sandwiches with
    Caramelized Onions, 63
  Chocolate Panini, 43
  PB and J Cutouts, 35
  Turkey Finger Sandwiches, 35
Sauces. See also Desserts/Sauces; Salsa.
  Red Pepper Romesco, 27
Scallop Ceviche, 63
Shrimp and Benne Seed Tartlets, 56
Soups. See also Chowder, Stew.
  Cauliflower Bisque, 18
  Chicken Soup with Lime and Cilantro,
    Caribbean-Style, 75
  Onion and Mushroom Bisque,
    Caramelized, 44
  Potato-Leek Soup, 23
Spinach
  Spanakopita, Deep-Dish, 69
  Tarts, Spinach and Gruyère, 49
Spread, Blue Cheese, 64
Spread, Pink Princess, 37
Squash Mash, Butternut, 15
Squash with Candied Pecans, Maple
  Mashed, 32
Stew with Rosemary Croutons,
  Oyster, 30
Sweet Potatoes
  Biscuits, Sweet Potato-Butter
    Pecan, 78
  Casserole, Sweet Potato, 74
  Salad with Bacon Vinaigrette, Sweet
    Potato, 59

Tacos, Carnita, 82
Trout and Pecan Crostini, Smoked, 12
Turkey
  Roast Turkey with Cider-Rosemary
    Gravy, 20
  Sandwiches, Turkey Finger, 35
  Sausage Patties, Turkey, 49

Vegetables. See also specific types.
  Lasagna, Roasted Vegetable, 70
  Succotash with Gruyère Grits,
    Autumn, 47

General Index

Birdhouses, 116–117

Cake stands, 102, 155–157
candle decorations, 92–97, 104–105, 110, 126–128, 140–141
centerpieces, 101–102, 104, 108, 115, 119, 123, 130, 132–133, 151–157
Christmas trees, 98, 139, 144–145

Decorating ideas
chic cottage look, 98–103
earthy color scheme, 104–109
garden inspiration, 110–117, 120, 124–125, 129
ornaments, 104–109, 118–119, 124–125, 154
plant containers, 124
using plates, 134–137

Floral decorations, 102, 110–111, 113, 118–119, 123–125, 134–135, 146, 155

Garlands, 98–99, 117–119, 124–125, 150
gift ideas, 145, 162, 164–165

gift-wrapping ideas, 90–91, 98–100, 110–111, 116, 139, 144–145, 147–149, 152, 155–157, 167
guest-room ideas, 144–145

How-to projects
floral centerpiece, 151–152, 154–155
frame stars, 140
gift tags, 167
grow your own bulbs, 113
lampshades, 160–161
magnolia place mats, 115
ornament collections, 153
party decorating, 155–157
pillows, 158–159
tie a package bow, 149
tiers of fruit, 153
wine caddy centerpiece, 123
wreath, 126–127, 149

Invitations, 163, 166

Lampshade decorating ideas, 144–145, 160–161

Mantels, 92–99, 105–107, 119, 130–131, 136–137, 140–141

Party-favor ideas, 109, 114, 121, 132
pinecones, 106–107, 124, 136–137
place-card ideas, 18–19, 31, 132–133
place mats, 114–115

Seasonal decorating, 92–97
stockings, 90, 98–100, 106–107, 121, 145

Table decorations, 101–105, 108–109, 119, 130, 132–133, 151–157
trees, 112–113, 115, 128, 130–131

Window decorations, 124–129, 142
wreaths
berries, 148, 155–157
feathers, 138
fresh flowers, 119
evergreen, 98–99, 110–113, 117
hydrangea bloom, 99
leaves, 92–97
magnolia, 93
pinecones, 117
ribbon, 110–113
star, 143
wheatgrass, 126–127

Contributors

Editorial Contributors

Lauren Brooks	Alicia Frazier
Teddie Butcher	Susan Huff
Adrienne Davis	Katie Stoddard
Catherine Fowler	Linda Wright

Recipe Contributors

Margaret Agnew	Ana Kelly
Rebecca Boggan	Jackie Mills
Jennifer Cofield	Elizabeth Taliaferro
Lorrie Hulston Corvin	

Thanks to the following homeowners

Katherine and Garry Ard	Lori and Peter Reich
Ann and Russell Chambliss	Tracy and John Runnion
Jennifer and Bobby Given	Tammy and Tim Stone
Susan and Don Huff	Sally and Jeff Threlkeld
Mallie and George Lynn	Robert Vandrell
Kay and Tom Merrill	Linda Wright
Vickie and David Rader	

Thanks to these Birmingham businesses

A'Mano	Lamb's Ears Ltd.
Angels Cake & Confections	Mulberry Heights Antiques
Bromberg & Co.	Rosegate
Christine's	Table Matters
Christmas & Co./FlowerBuds, Inc.	The Christmas Tree
Davis Wholesale Florist	Tricia's Treasures
Flora	

Special thanks

Seasons of Cannon Falls™
Cannon Falls, Minnesota

Sugar Mountain Nursery & Landscape
Newland, North Carolina

holiday planner

Start the season off right by getting organized early. Use the following pages to record parties and events on the planning calendars, prepare your home for holiday celebrations, and keep lists of all the items you'll need to make this season unforgettable.

planning calendar for November 178

planning calendar for December 180

10 quick tips for decorating success 182

crafting for the holidays 183

party planner 184

entertaining guide 186

Christmas dinner planner 187

gifts and greetings 188

holiday memories 190

looking ahead 192

November

Sunday	Monday	Tuesday	Wednesday
			1
5	6	7	8
12	13	14	15
19	20	21	22
26	27	28	29

2006

Thursday	Friday	Saturday
2	3	4
9	10	11
16	17	18
Thanksgiving 23	24	25
30		

seasonal essentials

Start stocking up on these items early.

- ☐ Greeting cards
- ☐ Party invitations
- ☐ Stamps
- ☐ Assorted gift boxes and bags
- ☐ Wrapping paper
- ☐ Tissue paper
- ☐ Ribbons and bows
- ☐ Tape
- ☐ Gift tags
- ☐ Seasonal fruits
- ☐ Mixed nuts
- ☐ Assorted chocolates
- ☐ Baking ingredients
- ☐ Seasonal table linens, napkins, and dish towels
- ☐ Candles
- ☐ Wreaths and garlands

things to do

December

Sunday	Monday	Tuesday	Wednesday
3	4	5	6
10	11	12	13
17	18	19	20
24 Christmas Eve / New Year's Eve 31	Christmas 25	26	27

2006

Thursday	Friday	Saturday
	1	2
7	8	9
14	15	16
21	22	23
28	29	30

holiday-ready pantry

Get prepared for the holidays by keeping these items on hand.

- ☐ Assorted coffees, teas, hot chocolate, and eggnog
- ☐ Wine, beer, and soft drinks
- ☐ White, brown, and powdered sugars
- ☐ Ground allspice, cinnamon, cloves, ginger, and nutmeg
- ☐ Seasonal fresh herbs
- ☐ Baking chocolate
- ☐ Semisweet morsels
- ☐ Assorted nuts
- ☐ Flaked coconut
- ☐ Sweetened condensed milk
- ☐ Whipping cream
- ☐ Jams, jellies, and preserves
- ☐ Raisins, cranberries, and other fresh or dried fruits
- ☐ Canned pumpkin
- ☐ Frozen/refrigerated bread dough, biscuits, and croissants
- ☐ Ice

things to do

10 quick tips for decorating success

Here are some quick, inexpensive ways to bring holiday cheer into your home.

1. **Use glass bowls or metallic platters** to display small candles for an illuminating effect throughout your home.

2. **Showcase infant Christmas dresses** from years past. Hang on padded hangers, and tie festive ribbons around the necks.

3. **Wrap grapevine wreaths with Christmas lights**, and hang them in windows.

4. **Use pomegranates, citrus fruits, and cranberries** to add seasonal color to wreaths, table arrangements, and mantel decorations.

5. **String silver-colored buttons** on heavy thread to create garland for the Christmas tree. Use large glass beads for spacing between the buttons.

6. **Enhance a simple container** of evergreen foliage by placing a mirror underneath. Arrange glittery ornaments at the base of the container to complete the setting.

7. **Tie ribbons on holiday cookie cutters**, and hang them in varying lengths in your kitchen windows.

8. **Purchase several votive candles** in a holiday scent—such as sugar cookie, cinnamon, or gingerbread—to make your home as fragrant as Santa's kitchen.

9. **Give traditional Christmas decorations a twist** by using a blue-and-white theme.

10. **Create a theme tree** to display favorite collectibles. For example, if you have a passion for the sea, adorn your tree with seashells and other nautical embellishments.

Decorating To-do List

Make your list and check it twice for stress-free decorating.

Gather materials

from the yard ....

....

from around the house ....

....

from the store ....

....

other ....

....

Add holiday decorations

to the table ....

....

to the door ....

....

to the mantel ....

....

to the staircase ....

....

other ....

....

crafting for the holidays

Go beyond baking cookies, and create an assortment of holiday cards, gift boxes, tags, baskets, and ornaments to show your creative spirit. These lists help you get started.

Kids' Crafts and Activities

These ideas allow your children to experience
the spirit of the season.

• **Let each child have a tree in his or her room.** Allow kids to decorate with a variety of ribbons and lights, and include 24 wrapped candy canes on each tree. Count down to Christmas with your children by allowing them to remove one candy cane each day—starting on the first day of December—for an after-meal treat.

• **Give your children a chance to share holiday cheer** by creating handmade Christmas cards. These cards are sure to pass along the joy of the season.

• **Join your children in decorating or making ornaments** for gifts and for the family to hang on the tree.

• **Let little hands be helping hands.** Give your children the chance to become Santa's helpers by including them in the kitchen. Allow them to mix punches, add toppings to cookies and pies, and serve appetizers to family and friends.

• **Collect easy cookie recipes** that you can help your children mix, bake, and decorate. Be sure to include recipes that have sprinkles, frostings, and other sweet additions.

• **Feature a child's tea set on a small table,** inviting little guests to celebrate the holiday in their own special way.

• **Have your children fill glass jars** with an assortment of holiday candies to give as teacher gifts. Let them decorate the outside of the jars with a variety of festive stickers; then tie a ribbon around each lid, and attach a gift tag.

Holiday Craft Supplies

Keep this supply of craft materials handy
to personalize gifts this Christmas.

- Beads
- Buttons
- Braids
- Lace
- Fringe
- Glitter
- Rhinestones
- Sequins
- Ribbons
- Twine
- Scrapbook paper
- Hole punch
- Assorted die-cut punches
- Craft glue
- Craft knife
- Craft paint
- Markers
- Cookie cutters
- Felt squares
- Puffy paint

Gift-Wrapping Supplies

Make sure these items are available
to wrap up the holidays in style.

- Assorted gift boxes
- Clear bags
- Buckets
- Baskets
- Tissue paper
- Cellophane
- Patterned and solid wrapping paper
- Vellum
- Wax paper
- Double-sided tape
- Satin tape
- Ribbons
- Bows
- Seasonal stickers
- Paintbrushes or foam brushes
- Spray artificial snow
- Glue gun and glue sticks
- Scissors

party planner

Everyone has a favorite recipe that they enjoy bringing to the table. Keep track of who's bringing what to your big get-together this year with the following chart.

guests	what they're bringing	serving pieces needed
	☐appetizer ☐beverage ☐bread ☐main dish ☐side dish ☐dessert	
	☐appetizer ☐beverage ☐bread ☐main dish ☐side dish ☐dessert	
	☐appetizer ☐beverage ☐bread ☐main dish ☐side dish ☐dessert	
	☐appetizer ☐beverage ☐bread ☐main dish ☐side dish ☐dessert	
	☐appetizer ☐beverage ☐bread ☐main dish ☐side dish ☐dessert	
	☐appetizer ☐beverage ☐bread ☐main dish ☐side dish ☐dessert	
	☐appetizer ☐beverage ☐bread ☐main dish ☐side dish ☐dessert	
	☐appetizer ☐beverage ☐bread ☐main dish ☐side dish ☐dessert	
	☐appetizer ☐beverage ☐bread ☐main dish ☐side dish ☐dessert	
	☐appetizer ☐beverage ☐bread ☐main dish ☐side dish ☐dessert	
	☐appetizer ☐beverage ☐bread ☐main dish ☐side dish ☐dessert	
	☐appetizer ☐beverage ☐bread ☐main dish ☐side dish ☐dessert	
	☐appetizer ☐beverage ☐bread ☐main dish ☐side dish ☐dessert	
	☐appetizer ☐beverage ☐bread ☐main dish ☐side dish ☐dessert	
	☐appetizer ☐beverage ☐bread ☐main dish ☐side dish ☐dessert	
	☐appetizer ☐beverage ☐bread ☐main dish ☐side dish ☐dessert	
	☐appetizer ☐beverage ☐bread ☐main dish ☐side dish ☐dessert	
	☐appetizer ☐beverage ☐bread ☐main dish ☐side dish ☐dessert	

Guest List

Use the following lines to record your party invitation list.
Be sure to include addresses and phone numbers.

Pantry List

Remind yourself of what you have and
what you still need to buy.

Party To-do List

Jot down reminders to keep things
running smoothly.

entertaining guide
The holidays are the perfect time to welcome friends, family, and guests into your home. These entertaining tips make everyone feel welcome.

Instant Entertaining Success
Use these quick fixes with unexpected and short-notice guests.

• **Stock your refrigerator** with an assortment of ready-to-eat vegetables, such as carrots, celery, cherry tomatoes, and broccoli. Pair with a veggie dip or salad dressing for a quick appetizer.

• **Arrange a variety of soft cheeses and crackers** on a glass pedestal or holiday platter. Add cranberries or sliced apples for a festive look.

• **Prepare quick bean dip** by layering refried beans, salsa, guacamole, and sour cream; top with grated Cheddar cheese, black olives, and chopped tomatoes and green onions.

• **Create last-minute appetizers** by toasting thinly sliced baguettes topped with marinated tomato slices and shredded mozzarella.

Prepare for the Best
Get the upper hand in the kitchen by planning ahead.

• **Keep an assortment of mini desserts**—such as sweet breads, brownie cups, and other favorite treats—available in your freezer. These goodies can be conveniently thawed at room temperature, in the toaster oven, or in the microwave.

• **Make your favorite casserole** the day before it is needed, and store it in the refrigerator up to 24 hours before cooking and serving. Or after baking the casserole, store it in the freezer to be eaten at a later date.

• **Keep extra shredded cheese** in your freezer to be used as a last-minute topper for side dishes and entrées.

• **Stock your freezer with premade phyllo shells** that can be filled with anything from instant lemon pudding to sweetened cream cheese.

Guest List
Write your Christmas dinner invitation list. Include addresses and phone numbers.

....
....
....
....
....
....
....
....
....
....
....
....
....
....
....
....
....
....

Christmas dinner planner
Jazz up the traditional feast by introducing new recipes along with the favorites. Use these lists for smooth planning.

Menu Ideas
Plan what you want to serve by looking at recipes from the past and new ideas you've found this season.

Dinner To-do List
Plan ahead for a successful event.

gifts and greetings

Keep these pages handy when making your Christmas card and gift lists this year. Use the size charts on the following page to guarantee perfect fit.

Christmas Card List

name	address	sent/received

Gift List and Size Charts

         gift purchased/made   sent/delivered

name ....

jeans_____ shirt_____ sweater_____ jacket_____ shoes_____ belt_____

blouse_____ skirt_____ slacks_____ dress_____ suit_____ coat_____

pajamas_____ robe_____ hat_____ gloves_____ ring_____

name ....

jeans_____ shirt_____ sweater_____ jacket_____ shoes_____ belt_____

blouse_____ skirt_____ slacks_____ dress_____ suit_____ coat_____

pajamas_____ robe_____ hat_____ gloves_____ ring_____

name ....

jeans_____ shirt_____ sweater_____ jacket_____ shoes_____ belt_____

blouse_____ skirt_____ slacks_____ dress_____ suit_____ coat_____

pajamas_____ robe_____ hat_____ gloves_____ ring_____

name ....

jeans_____ shirt_____ sweater_____ jacket_____ shoes_____ belt_____

blouse_____ skirt_____ slacks_____ dress_____ suit_____ coat_____

pajamas_____ robe_____ hat_____ gloves_____ ring_____

name ....

jeans_____ shirt_____ sweater_____ jacket_____ shoes_____ belt_____

blouse_____ skirt_____ slacks_____ dress_____ suit_____ coat_____

pajamas_____ robe_____ hat_____ gloves_____ ring_____

name ....

jeans_____ shirt_____ sweater_____ jacket_____ shoes_____ belt_____

blouse_____ skirt_____ slacks_____ dress_____ suit_____ coat_____

pajamas_____ robe_____ hat_____ gloves_____ ring_____

name ....

jeans_____ shirt_____ sweater_____ jacket_____ shoes_____ belt_____

blouse_____ skirt_____ slacks_____ dress_____ suit_____ coat_____

pajamas_____ robe_____ hat_____ gloves_____ ring_____

name ....

jeans_____ shirt_____ sweater_____ jacket_____ shoes_____ belt_____

blouse_____ skirt_____ slacks_____ dress_____ suit_____ coat_____

pajamas_____ robe_____ hat_____ gloves_____ ring_____

holiday memories
Remember your favorite moments from this year by preserving them here.

Treasured Traditions
Highlight your favorite holiday traditions on these lines.

Special Holiday Activities
Record events you attended this year and begin your list of those you want to attend next year.

Holiday Visits and Visitors

Remember whom you celebrated with this year, what gifts were given, and any updates, such as marriages and births.

....
....
....
....
....
....
....
....
....
....
....
....
....
....
....
....
....
....
....
....
....
....
....
....
....
....
....
....
....
....
....
....
....
....
....

This Year's Favorite Recipes

Appetizers and Beverages ....
....
....
....
....

Entrées ....
....
....
....

Sides and Salads ....
....
....
....

Cookies and Candies ....
....
....
....

Desserts ....
....
....
....

looking ahead

Holiday Wrap-up

Make a list of thank-you notes to be sent for gifts and holiday hospitality.

Notes for Next Year

Begin collecting ideas for Christmas 2007 by making notes about changes you'd like to make
or traditions you'd like to continue next year.